The **ESSE............** of

Intermediate
Accounting II

Eldon R. Bailey, Ph.D.
Chairperson, Department of Accounting
McNeese State University, Louisiana

> This book is a continuation of *"THE ESSENTIALS OF INTERMEDIATE ACCOUNTING I"* and begins with Chapter 9. It covers the usual course outline of Intermediate Accounting II. Earlier/basic topics are covered in *"THE ESSENTIALS OF INTERMEDIATE ACCOUNTING I."*

Research & Education Association
61 Ethel Road West
Piscataway, New Jersey 08854

THE ESSENTIALS®
OF INTERMEDIATE ACCOUNTING II

Printed in the United States of America

Library of Congress Catalog Card Number 98-67285

International Standard Book Number 0-87891-683-0

WHAT "THE ESSENTIALS" WILL DO FOR YOU

This book is a review and study guide. It is comprehensive and it is concise.

It helps in preparing for exams, in doing homework, and remains a handy reference source at all times.

It condenses the vast amount of detail characteristic of the subject matter and summarizes the **essentials** of the field.

It will thus save hours of study and preparation time.

The book provides quick access to the important facts, principles, theorems, concepts, and equations in the field.

Materials needed for exams can be reviewed in summary form – eliminating the need to read and re-read many pages of textbook and class notes. The summaries will even tend to bring detail to mind that had been previously read or noted.

This "ESSENTIALS" book has been prepared by an expert in the field, and has been carefully reviewed to assure accuracy and maximum usefulness.

Dr. Max Fogiel
Program Director

CONTENTS

This book is a continuation of *"THE ESSENTIALS OF INTERMEDIATE ACCOUNTING I"* and begins with Chapter 9. It covers the usual course outline of Intermediate Accounting II. Earlier/basic topics are covered in *"THE ESSENTIALS OF INTERMEDIATE ACCOUNTING I"*.

CHAPTER 9

CURRENT LIABILITIES

Liabilities are defined by the FASB(Financial Accounting Standards Board) in **Concepts Statement No. 6** as "probable future sacrifices of economic benefits arising from present obligations of a particular entity to transfer assets or provide services to other entities in the future as the result of past transactions or events." **Current liabilities** are those which are expected to be paid using current assets or through creation of other current liabilities. In conformity with the definition of current assets, current liabilities are those expected to be paid within the operating cycle or one year, whichever is longer. Other liabilities are classified as **long-term liabilities.**

Liabilities are recognized in accounting when they are incurred. The amount to be recognized usually is the amount payable at the due date of the liability.

9.1 TYPES OF CURRENT LIABILITIES

ACCOUNTS PAYABLE

Trade accounts payable are liabilities that arise from the purchase of goods and services on open account in the course of the entity's ongoing central operations. Accounting for accounts payable generally parallels that of accounts receivable, discussed in Chapter 4 of *Essentials of Intermediate Accounting I.*

SHORT-TERM NOTES PAYABLE

A **note payable** is a written promise to pay a specified amount of money at a designated time. Short-term notes payable typically originate from the purchase of goods or services or the borrowing of money.

For example, assume a company purchases equipment costing $5,000 and issues a note bearing interest at the rate of 12%, payable in six months. The note is dated October 1 and the company's accounting period ends December 31.

Oct. 1	Equipment	5,000	
	Notes Payable		5,000
Dec. 31	Interest Expense		
	($5,000 x 12% x 3/12)	150	
	Interest Payable		150
Apr. 1	Notes Payable	5,000	
	Interest Expense	150	
	Interest Payable	150	
	Cash		5,300

The April 1 entry assumes that no reversing entry was made.

To illustrate money borrowed from a bank on a discount basis, assume that a company issues a noninterest-bearing note with a face value of $5,000 to a bank which discounts it at 12%. The note is dated October 1 and is due in six months.

Discount = $5,000 x 12% x 1/2 year = $300
Proceeds = $5,000 - $300 = $4,700

Oct. 1	Cash	4,700	
	Discount on Notes Payable	300	
	Notes Payable		5,000
Dec. 31	Interest Expense	150	
	Discount on Notes Payable		150
	($300 x 3/6)		
Apr. 1	Interest Expense	150	
	Notes Payable	5,000	
	Discount on Notes Payable		150
	Cash		5,000

Current maturities of long-term notes payable, due during the next year or operating cycle, whichever is longer, should be classified as current liabilities unless they are payable from a sinking fund classified as a long-term investment.

SHORT-TERM DEBT EXPECTED TO BE REFINANCED

A company may plan to refinance certain short-term debt on a long-term basis. Such short-term debt should be excluded from current liabilities if the following conditions are met: (1) there is **intent** on the part of the entity to refinance on a long-term basis, and (2) the entity has the **ability** to refinance. **SFAS 6** provides guidance in interpreting these conditions.

Current liabilities may be paid using current assets after the balance sheet date, with the current assets subsequently being replaced through the issuance of long-term debt. Such current liabilities should **not** be classified as long-term but should be included in current liabilities at the balance sheet date.

DIVIDENDS PAYABLE

When the board of directors of a corporation declares a cash or property dividend, the dividend becomes a current liability of the corporation if it is payable within one year or the operating cycle, whichever is longer.

ADVANCES FROM CUSTOMERS

A company may receive refundable deposits from customers or advance payments for goods or services. Such payments should be reported as liabilities until refunded or until the goods or services are provided.

For example, assume a company received an order for manufacture of products with a total selling price of $100,000. The company requires a 25% deposit on such special orders.

Entry for receipt of deposit:

Cash	25,000	
Advances from Customers		25,000

Entry for delivery of goods:

Accounts Receivable	75,000	
Advances from Customers	25,000	
Sales		100,000

TAX LIABILITIES

Sales Taxes. Many jurisdictions require sellers to collect sales taxes on sales and remit these taxes to the government. Sales taxes so collected should be reported as liabilities until remitted to the government. Some governments allow sellers to keep a small percentage of the sales taxes collected as compensation for the collection of the taxes.

ILLUSTRATION:

A sale is made where the sales tax rate is 5%.

Accounts Receivable	1,050	
Sales		1,000
Sales Taxes Payable		50

Sales taxes are remitted monthly to the government, with a 1% fee to the sellers. Assume total sales taxes collected in January are $5,000. The entry in February for payment of the taxes:

Sales Taxes Payable	5,000	
Cash		4,950
Miscellaneous Revenue		50

Property Taxes. Property taxes are generally levied against the assessed value of real and personal property. Such taxes are usually collected once a year and become payable on a specified due date.

Property taxes should be recognized as an expense equally over the months of the taxing period to which they apply. In some cases it may be necessary to estimate the property tax expense for months before the tax bill is received.

EXAMPLE

Assume a company's accounting period ends on December 31. The taxing period for property taxes is July 1 - June 30. The tax bill is mailed in November, with a due date of December 31.

For the months July through October, the following monthly accruals are made, based on an estimate of total property taxes for the July 1 - June 30 year of $9,000:

Property Taxes Expense	750	
Property Taxes Payable		750

The tax bill is received and paid in November. The actual total tax for the tax year was $9,080.

Property Taxes Payable	3,000	
Prepaid Property Taxes	6,080	
Cash		9,080

For each of the remaining months, November through June, a monthly adjusting entry would be made:

| Property Taxes Expense($6,080/8 months) | 760 | |
| Prepaid Property Taxes Expense | | 760 |

Payroll Taxes. The federal government and most state governments require income taxes and other taxes to be withheld by employers from employee pay. These governments also levy taxes against employers on the basis of employee pay. Taxes required to be withheld include federal income tax, state income tax, and Social Security (FICA) taxes. Taxes levied against employers include a matching Social Security tax and unemployment taxes. Employees may also authorize voluntary deductions for items such as insurance and union dues. Amounts withheld from employee pay and related employer payroll taxes should be reported as current liabilities until paid.

EXAMPLE

Assume the following payroll data:

Gross pay	22,000
Federal income tax withheld	1,760
FICA tax withheld	1,652
Employee insurance premiums withheld	880
Employee union dues withheld	210
Federal unemployment tax	66
State unemployment tax	770

Entry to record payroll:

Salaries and Wages Expense	22,000	
Federal Withholding Tax Payable		1,760
FICA Taxes Payable		1,652
Employee Insurance Premiums Payable		880
Employee Union Dues Payable		210
Cash		17,498

Entry to record employer's payroll taxes (employer's matching FICA contribution plus the federal and state unemployment taxes):

Payroll Taxes Expense	2,488	
FICA Taxes Payable		1,652
Federal Unemployment Taxes Payable		66
State Unemployment Taxes Payable		770

Bonuses. Some companies award bonuses to key employees as additional compensation. Such bonuses are often based on company income for a specified period. Bonuses should be recognized as expenses and liabilities when earned. Several methods of calculating bonuses are found in practice. Two such methods are illustrated below.

ILLUSTRATION

Assume a bonus of 6% of company net income after deducting the bonus but before deducting income tax. Company net income before the bonus is $180,000.

Bonus = .06($180,000 – Bonus)
Bonus = $10,800 – .06 Bonus
1.06 Bonus = $10,800
Bonus = $10,800 / 1.06
Bonus = $10,189 (Rounded)

Proof: Bonus = .06($180,000 – $10,189)
             Bonus = .06($169,811) = $10,189

ILLUSTRATION

Assume a bonus of 6% of company net income after deducting the bonus and income tax. Company net income before the bonus and taxes is $180,000. The company's income tax rate is 40%.

Bonus = .06($180,000 – Bonus – Taxes)
Taxes = .40($180,000 – Bonus)

Therefore:

Bonus = .06[$180,000 – Bonus – .40($180,000 – Bonus)]
Bonus = .06($180,000 – Bonus – $72,000 + .40 Bonus)
Bonus = .06($108,000 – .60 Bonus)
Bonus = $6,480 – .036 Bonus

1.036 Bonus = $6,480
Bonus = $6,480 / 1.036
Bonus = $6,255 (Rounded)

Proof: Taxes = .40($180,000 – $6,255)
            Taxes = .40($173,745) = $69,498
            Bonus = .06($180,000 – $6,255 – $69,498)
            Bonus = .06($104,247) = $6,255 (Rounded)

Entry to record bonus:

| Bonus Expense | 6,255 | |
| Bonuses Payable | | 6,255 |

9.2   ESTIMATED AND CONTINGENT LIABILITIES

A **contingency** is a situation involving a possible gain or loss, with the uncertainty being resolved when future events occur or fail to occur. **Loss contingencies** involve the incurrence of a liability or impairment of assets. The accounting standards define three conditions of the probability of future events confirming a loss: **Probable, reasonably possible,** and **remote.**

If a loss is believed to have incurred, it is probable that future events will confirm the loss, and the amount of the loss is reasonably estimable; the loss should be accrued and an **estimated liability** recognized. A contingent loss that is reasonably possible, even if the amount cannot be estimated, must be disclosed. Accounting standards do not require disclosure of a remote loss contingency.

WARRANTY OBLIGATIONS

Many companies offer warranties on products sold, requiring repair or replacement for products that fail within a specified period. Such warranties constitute a loss contingency. If the amount of expense to be incurred in honoring warranties can be estimated, it should be accrued and an estimated liability recognized.

ILLUSTRATION

Assume a company has sold products during a year totaling $1,000,000. Past experience and other information permit an estimate of expected warranty expense of $20,000 relating to these sales.

Accrual entry:

Warranty Expense	20,000	
Estimated Liability for Warranties		20,000

Entry for replacement of defective unit of product:

Estimated Liability for Warranties	500	
Inventory		500

PREMIUMS

Some companies offer premiums to purchasers of their products. The premiums usually will be awarded upon presentation of coupons, box tops, or the like. The expense associated with providing these premiums should be matched with the sales giving rise to the premium claims.

ILLUSTRATION

Assume a company sold products in 19x1 with an offer of a premium upon the return of a specified number of box tops. The company estimates that 20,000 premiums will be redeemed on the basis of 19x1 sales. The company acquires an inventory of the premiums at a cost of $2.50 each. The premium offer expires in 19x2. Actual premiums redeemed are 9,600 in 19x1 and 10,300 in 19x2 through the expiration date.

Entry to record acquisition of inventory:

Inventory of Premiums	50,000	
Cash		50,000

Entry to record issuance of premiums in 19x1:

Premium Expense (9,600 x $2.50)	24,000	
Inventory of Premiums		24,000

Entry to accrue estimated additional premium expense relating to 19x1 sales:

Premium Expense [(20,000 - 9,600) x $2.50]	26,000	
Estimated Liability for Premiums		26,000

Entry in 19x2 to record issuance of additional premiums:

Estimated Liability for Premiums (10,300 x $2.50)	25,750	
Inventory of Premiums		25,750

The remaining liability results from the difference between estimated and actual redemptions. It would be written off as an adjustment to Premium Expense in 19x2, as a change in accounting estimate.

Estimated Liability for Premiums	250	
Premium Expense		250

COMPENSATED ABSENCES

Many companies grant employees time off from work with pay, for example, vacation time. Generally accepted accounting principles require that the expense for such compensated absences be recognized in the period in which it is earned. If there is a carryover of unused vacation or other compensated absence time beyond the year in which it is earned, an accrual must be made if certain conditions are met. The conditions are: (1) the services for which the absence is earned have already been rendered, (2) the carryover is a vested right that accumulates, (3) the payment of compensation for future absences is probable, and (4) the amount of future payment can be reliably estimated.

ILLUSTRATION

Assume that at the end of year 19x1 the estimated compensation to be paid in the future for vacation time earned by employees in 19x1 but not taken is $28,000.

Wages and Salary Expense	28,000	
Liability for Vacation Pay		28,000

Assume that during 19x2 carryover vacation time is taken resulting in payment of wages and salaries of $26,000.

Liability for Vacation Pay	26,000	
Cash		26,000

LITIGATION

A contingent loss may arise when a company has been sued. Theoretically, if management believes that it is probable that the suit will be lost and the amount of damages can be reasonably estimated, the loss should be accrued and an estimated liability recognized. Management is likely to resist such an accrual since it may be regarded as an admission of guilt which would prejudice the company's case in court. Footnote disclosure is the more likely treatment of a contingent loss from a lawsuit.

CHAPTER 10

LONG-TERM LIABILITIES

Liabilities which do not qualify as current liabilities are classified as **long-term liabilities**. These liabilities are **not** expected to be paid within one year or the operating cycle, whichever is longer.

10.1 BONDS AND LONG-TERM NOTES

Bonds are long-term debt in which units of the debt are represented by bond certificates. The **issuer** of the bonds borrows from the lender(s), who receive the bond certificates as evidence of the debt. The document containing the provisions applicable to all bonds in an issue is called the **bond indenture**. For example, a company may borrow $10,000,000 with an issue consisting of 10,000 bonds of $1,000 each. The bond indenture would specify the interest rate, maturity date and other features of the bond issue.

In an issue of **term bonds**, all bonds mature on the same date. In a **serial bond** issue, bonds mature in installments at scheduled times. Interest and principal payments on **registered bonds** are paid to the registered owner of the bonds. Interest payments on **coupon** or **bearer bonds** are made to the party submitting interest coupons which are detached from the bond certificate. **Callable bonds** give the issuer the option of retiring the bonds before maturity at a specified call price. **Convertible bonds** give the lender the option of converting the bonds into shares of stock.

ISSUANCE OF BONDS

Bonds have a fixed **face, par,** or **maturity value**. Interest is payable on the bonds at a fixed **stated interest rate**. The amount of money received by an issuer at the time of issuance of bonds will depend on how market interest rates at that time compare to the stated interest rate on the bonds. If market interest rates are higher than the stated interest rates, the bonds will sell for less than their face value, or at a **discount**. If market rates are lower than the stated interest rates, the bonds will sell for more than their face value, or at a **premium**. The selling price will be that which provides a **yield** on the bonds equal to the market rate of interest. The periodic **cash interest payments** on bonds are based on the stated interest rate and the face value. The **interest expense** recognized is based on the market rate at the date of issuance of the bonds.

The price at which a bond issue sells is the present value of the future cash flows associated with the bonds. These cash flows are the interest payments and the maturity value. These cash flows are discounted at the market interest rate (yield rate) to determine the selling price.

ILLUSTRATION

Assume a bond issue with a face value of $1,000,000. Interest at the rate of 10% is payable annually. The bonds mature in ten years. The market rate of interest is 9%.

Issue price of bonds = Present value of interest payments and maturity value discounted at 9%

Interest payments = 10 annual payments of $100,000 (10% x $1,000,000)

Maturity value = $1,000,000 payable in ten years

Issue price = PV (10 annual payments of $100,000 discounted at 9%) + PV ($1,000,000 at end of 10 years discounted at 9%)

= 6.41766 ($100,000) + 0.422411 ($1,000,000)
= $641,766 + $422,411
= $1,064,177

Thus, the bonds will sell at a premium because the market interest rate is lower than the stated interest rate.

110

The entry to record the issuance of bonds consists of a debit to Cash, a credit to Bonds Payable, and either a debit to Discount on Bonds Payable or a credit to Premium on Bonds Payable. A discount account is contra to and a premium account is an adjunct to Bonds Payable. A discount balance is reported on the balance sheet as a deduction from Bonds Payable while a premium balance is added to Bonds Payable.

The entry for the bonds in the previous illustration would be:

Cash	1,064,177	
Bonds Payable		1,000,000
Premium on Bonds Payable		64,177

The term of a bond issue and the interest payment dates are fixed. However, the bonds may be sold between interest dates. The buyers of the bonds would pay for the interest accrued on the bonds since the start of the term of the bonds or the last interest payment date.

ILLUSTRATION

Assume a $1,000,000 bond issue, interest payable semian-nually at an annual rate of 10%. The bonds are dated June 1. The bonds are sold on July 1 at face value plus accrued interest.

Accrued interest = $1,000,000 x 10% x 1/12
= $8,333

Entry to record issuance of bonds:

Cash	1,008,333	
Bonds Payable		1,000,000
Interest Expense		8,333

The entry to record the interest payment on December 1 would be:

Interest Expense	50,000	
($1,000,000 x 10% x 6/12)		
Cash		50,000

The balance of the Interest Expense account after the December 1 interest payment would be $41,667 ($50,000 – $8,333), which repre-sents five months interest on the bonds (July 1 – December 1).

Bond issue costs are costs associated with the issuance of bonds, such as legal fees and printing and engraving costs. These costs should be recorded as Deferred Bond Issue Costs (an asset) and amortized as expense over the life of the bond issue by the straight-line method.

RECORDING INTEREST EXPENSE

Interest expense is recognized on a bond issue on the basis of the market interest rate (yield) at the time of issue. This recognition is accomplished in accounting through the amortization of any premium or discount on the issue. Amortization should be calculated using the **effective interest method.**

ILLUSTRATION

Assume a bond issue with a face value of $100,000, a stated interest rate of 12% annual rate, interest payable semiannually on June 30 and December 31. The bonds were sold at an effective interest rate (yield) of 10%. The issue price was $107,721. The term is 5 years.

Premium amortization table using the effective interest method is shown on the following page.

The entry to record the first interest payment would be:

Bond interest Expense	5,386	
Premium on Bonds Payable	614	
Cash		6,000

To illustrate amortization of a discount, assume that the bonds in the preceding illustration were issued for $92,976 to yield 14%.

Discount amortization table using the effective interest method is shown on the following page.

The entry for the first interest payment:

Bond Interest Expense	6,508	
Discount on Bonds Payable		508
Cash		6,000

Generally accepted accounting principles require the use of the effective interest method of amortization, except that another method may be used if the results are not materially different. Another method frequently used is the **straight-line method.** In this method the premium or discount is amortized in equal amounts over the remaining term of the bond issue.

Premium amortization table using the effective interest method.

(1) Interest Payment Number	(2) Cash Interest Paid (6% x $100,000)	(3) Interest Expense [5% x CV (col. 5)]	(4) Premium Amortization (2 – 3)	(5) Carrying Value (Prev. CV –4)
At issuance				$107,721
1	$6,000	$5,386	$614	107,107
2	6,000	5,355	645	106,462
3	6,000	5,323	677	105,785
4	6,000	5,289	711	105,074
5	6,000	5,254	746	104,328
6	6,000	5,216	784	103,544
7	6,000	5,177	823	102,721
8	6,000	5,136	864	101,857
9	6,000	5,093	907	100,950
10	6,000	5,050*	950*	100,000

* To amortize balance of premium. Not exact because of rounding.

Discount amortization table using the effective interest method.

(1) Interest Payment Number	(2) Cash Interest Paid (6% x $100,000)	(3) Interest Expense [7% x CV (col. 5)]	(4) Discount Amortization (2 – 3)	(5) Carrying Value (Prev. CV +4)
At issuance				$92,976
1	$6,000	$6,508	$508	93,484
2	6,000	6,544	544	94,028
3	6,000	6,582	582	94,610
4	6,000	6,623	623	95,233
5	6,000	6,666	666	95,899
6	6,000	6,713	713	96,612
7	6,000	6,763	763	97,375
8	6,000	6,816	816	98,191
9	6,000	6,873	873	99,064
10	6,000	6,936*	936*	100,000

* To amortize balance of discount. Not exact because of rounding.

For example, consider the illustration on page 113 in which bonds were issued at a discount of $100,000 − $92,976 = $7,024.

Straight-line amortization rate over 10 interest payment periods:

$7,024 / 10 = $702.40

The entry for each interest payment then would be:

Bond Interest Expense	6,702.40	
Discount on Bonds Payable		702.40
Cash		6,000.00

A company's accounting period often does not coincide with the interest payment dates of a bonds issue. Such a situation requires accrual of bond interest at the end of the accounting period.

As an illustration, again consider the bonds issued at a discount in the previous illustration. Assume that the interest payment dates are May 1 and November 1 and the firm's accounting period ends December 31.

Entry for interest payment number 1, November 1, 19x1:

Bond Interest Expense	6,508	
Discount on Bonds Payable		508
Cash		6,000

Accrual of bond interest on December 31, 19x1:

Bond Interest Expense ($6,544 x 2/6)	2,181	
Discount on Bonds Payable ($544 x 2/6)		181
Bond Interest Payable ($6,000 x 2/6)		2,000

Entry for interest payment on April 1, 19x2, assuming no reversing entries were made:

Bond Interest Expense ($6,544 − $2,181)	4,363	
Bond Interest Payable	2,000	
Discount on Bonds Payable ($544 − $181)		363
Cash		6,000

Serial bonds provide for payments on the principal of bonds in installments during the term of the bonds. Cash interest payments and amortization of premium or discount on serial bonds are calculated on the basis of bonds outstanding at a given time.

114

To illustrate, assume $300,000 face value of serial bonds are issued to yield 7% annually. The stated interest rate is 8%. Interest is payable semiannually. The bonds mature $100,000 at the end of the second, third, and fourth years. The bonds are sold for $307,937.

Amortization table for the effective interest method appears on Page 116.

The entry for the payments on the sixth interest date:

Bond Interest Expense	7,066	
Bonds Payable	100,000	
Premium on Bonds Payable	934	
Cash		108,000

BONDS WITH DETACHABLE STOCK WARRANTS

Bonds may be issued with **detachable stock warrants.** The warrants give the holder the option to purchase a specified number of shares of stock at a specified price. Since the warrants are detachable, they are considered a security separate from the bonds. Normally, after issuance of the bonds, the warrants will achieve a separate market value.

The proceeds from the issuance of bonds with detachable stock warrants must be divided between the bonds (debt) and the warrants (equity). The allocation of the proceeds is based on the relative separate market values of the bonds and warrants. If the warrants are **not detachable**, no portion of the proceeds should be allocated to the warrants.

ILLUSTRATION

Assume issuance of $1,000,000 face value of bonds for $1,030,000. Each $1,000 bond carries a warrant giving the holder the option to purchase 10 shares of stock at $40 per share. Shortly after issuance, the warrants and bonds sell separately for $50 and $990, respectively.

$$\text{Proceeds allocated to bonds} = \frac{\text{Market price of bonds}}{\text{Market price of bonds + warrants}} \times \$1,030$$

Amortization table showing effective interest method.

(1) Interest Payment Number	(2) Cash Interest Paid	(3) Interest Expense	(4) Premium Amortization	(5) Principal Payment	(6) Principal Outstanding	(7) Carrying Value
At issuance					$300,000	$307,937
1	$12,000	$10,778	$1,222	–	300,000	306,715
2	12,000	10,735	1,265	–	300,000	305,450
3	12,000	10,691	1,309	–	300,000	304,141
4	12,000	10,645	1,355	$100,000	200,000	202,786
5	8,000	7,098	902	–	200,000	201,884
6	8,000	7,066	934	100,000	100,000	100,950
7	4,000	3,533	467	–	100,000	100,483
8	4,000	3,517	483	100,000	–	–

(2) Principal outstanding previous line x 4%
(3) Carrying value previous line x $3^{1}/_{2}$%
(4) Col. 2 value – Col. 3 value
(6) Principal outstanding previous line – Col. 5 value
(7) Carrying value previous line – Col. 4 value – Col. 5 value

$$= \frac{\$990}{\$990 + \$50} \quad x \quad \$1,030$$

$$= \$980.48$$

Proceeds allocated to warrants = $1,030 – $980.48 = $49.52

Entry for issuance of bonds:

Cash	1,030,000	
Discount on Bonds Payable		
($1,000,000 – $980,480)	19,520	
Bonds Payable		1,000,000
Stock Warrants ($49.52 x 1,000)		49,520

The Stock Warrants account would be reported as paid-in capital.

Assume exercise of 6,000 of the warrants to purchase 6,000 shares of the company's $25 par value common stock:

Cash (6,000 x $40)	240,000	
Stock Warrants (600 x $49.52)	29,712	

116

Common Stock (6,000 x $25)		150,000
Paid-in Capital in Excess of Par		119,712

Assume the remaining warrants expire without being exercised:

Stock Warrants ($49,520 – $29,712)	19,808	
Additional Paid-in Capital from Expired Warrants		19,808

LONG-TERM NOTES PAYABLE

The accounting for notes payable that are classified as long-term generally parallels that for short-term notes payable, assuming the notes carry a stated fair interest rate.

Problems have arisen in accounting for transactions involving **noninterest-bearing** notes payable. **APB**(Accounting Principles Board) **Opinion 21** concludes that such notes in fact usually include an interest component which must be determined and accounted for.

Notes Issued for Cash. When long-term noninterest- bearing notes payable are issued for cash, the cash proceeds are assumed to equal the present value of the debt. The discount (or premium) is the difference between the present value and the face value. This discount or premium is to be amortized over the term of the note as interest expense by the effective interest method. The effective interest rate is that rate of interest which discounts the maturity value to equal the present value of the note.

ILLUSTRATION

Assume that on January 1, 19x1, a company exchanges a noninterest-bearing note with a face value of $10,000 for $7,513. The note is due in three years. The effective interest rate is calculated to be 10%.

Entry to record note:

Cash	7,513	
Discount on Notes Payable	2,487	
Notes Payable		10,000

Entry to record interest on December 31, 19x1:

Interest Expense (10% x $7,513)	751.30	
Discount on Notes Payable		751.30

The carrying value of the note on December 31, 19x1, becomes $8,264.30 ($7,513 + $751.30 or $10,000 − ($2,487 − $751.30)). The entry to record interest on December 31, 19x2:

Interest Expense (10% x $8,264.30)   826.43
Discount on Notes Payable   826.43

Notes Issued for Property, Goods, or Services. If a noninterest-bearing note is issued for property, goods, or services, the transaction is recorded at the fair market value of the property, goods, or services, or the fair market value of the note, whichever is more clearly determinable. This value is considered the present value of the note and an effective interest rate is calculated and interest expense recognized as with notes issued for cash. If neither the fair market value of the property, goods, or services nor of the note is determinable, the present value of the note is calculated using the borrower's incremental interest rate.

Notes Issued for Cash and Rights or Privileges. If a note issued for cash also involves special rights or privileges granted to the payee, the note is recorded at its present value using the incremental interest rate of the borrower. The difference between this present value and the cash received is unearned revenue associated with the special rights or privileges granted.

ILLUSTRATION

Assume a company borrows $50,000 cash from a customer and signs a noninterest-bearing note for that amount payable in two years. The company also grants the customer the right to purchase goods at reduced prices during that period. The company's incremental interest rate is 12%.

Present value of the note = $50,000 discounted for
                                            2 years at 12%
                                       = $39,860

Unearned revenue from sales = $50,000 − $39,860 = $10,140

Entry to record note:

Cash   50,000
Discount on Notes Payable   10,140

118

| Notes Payable | 50,000 | |
| Unearned Revenue | 10,140 | |

Entry to record interest at end of the first year:

| Interest Expense (12% x $39,860) | 4,783 | |
| Discount on Notes Payable | | 4,783 |

Assuming the customer agrees to purchase equal amounts of goods over the two-year period, the unearned revenue would be recognized as revenue equally over the two years. The adjustment at the end of each of the years would be:

| Unearned Revenue (1/2 x $10,140) | 5,070 | |
| Sales | | 5,070 |

10.2 RETIREMENT, REDEMPTION, AND CONVERSION

RETIREMENT AT MATURITY

At the maturity date of bonds or long-term notes, the carrying value will equal the face value since all premium or discount will have been amortized. At payment of the maturity value, Bonds Payable (or other liability account) will be debited and Cash credited for the face value of the debt.

RETIREMENT BEFORE MATURITY

Bonds or other long-term debt may be paid off (extinguished) before maturity through exercise of the call privilege or through purchase on the open market. The difference between the carrying value of the debt and the call price or market price at redemption is recognized as a loss or gain. Losses and gains from extinguishment of debt are to be reported as extraordinary items on the income statement.

DEFEASANCE

Long-term debt may be extinguished by (1) the debtor being released from liability by law or the creditor or (2) by the debtor placing assets in an irrevocable trust to be used solely for satisfaction of the debt (**in-substance defeasance**). In the first case, the debt should be removed from the accounts and an extraordinary gain recognized. In the case of in-substance defeasance, **SFAS 76** provides for recognition of an extraordinary gain or loss equal to the difference between the cost of the assets placed in trust and the carrying value of the debt. **SFAS 76** established specific requirements the trust must meet in order to consider the situation an extinguishment of debt.

CONVERTIBLE BONDS

Convertible bonds may be issued giving the holder the option to convert the bonds into stock. All of the proceeds from such bonds should be accounted for as debt. If bonds are converted, there are two methods which may be used to record the conversion. In the **book value method**, the carrying value of the bonds is considered the issue price of the stock, and no gain or loss is recognized on the conversion. In the **market value method**, the market value of the stock is used and a gain or loss recognized for any difference between the stock value and the carrying value of the bonds.

ILLUSTRATION

Assume bonds with a face value of $20,000 and unamortized discount of $620 are converted into 800 shares of common stock having a par value of $20 per share and a current market value of $30 per share.

The entry for the book value method:

Bonds Payable	20,000	
Discount on Bonds Payable		620
Common Stock (800 x $20)		16,000
Paid-in Capital in Excess of Par		
($20,000 − $620 − $16,000)		3,380

The entry if the market value method is used:

Bonds Payable	20,000	
Loss on Conversion of Bonds		
[(800 x $30) − ($20,000 − $620)]	4,620	
Discount on Bonds Payable		620
Common Stock (800 x $20)		16,000
Paid-in Capital in Excess of Par		
(800 x $10)		8,000

A company with convertible bonds outstanding may induce conversion by adding a "sweetener" in the form of revised conversion terms. **SFAS 84** requires that when conversion occurs in such a case, the debtor must recognize as expense the excess of the fair value of the stock and other consideration issued over the fair value of the stock issuable under the original conversion terms.

10.3 TROUBLED DEBT RESTRUCTURING

SFAS 15 states that a troubled debt restructuring occurs when a creditor, because of a debtor's financial difficulties, grants a concession that it would not otherwise consider. A restructuring may involve a modification of the terms of the debt or a transfer of asset or equity interest.

In a restructuring involving a modification of terms, two situations are possible: (1) Future cash payments may be greater than the face value plus accrued interest on the present debt. In this case, no gain is recognized, the carrying value of the debt is unchanged, and interest expense is recognized in the future using an imputed interest rate. The imputed interest rate is that rate which discounts the future cash payments to the carrying value of the debt. (2) Future cash payments may be less than the face value plus accrued interest on the present debt. A gain is recognized, the carrying value of the liability is reduced, and no interest expense is recognized in the future.

ILLUSTRATION: CASE 1

A company has a debt of $100,000 plus $11,000 accrued interest, which is currently due. The creditor agrees to extend the due date two years and reduce the interest rate from 14% to 12%, interest payable annually.

Future cash payments:

Interest: $100,000 x 12% x 2 years	$ 24,000
Principal payable in two years	100,000
Total	$124,000

Imputed interest rate = 6% (Present value of above cash payments discounted at 6% = $111,000)

Entry to restate Notes Payable to present value:

Interest Payable	11,000	
Notes Payable		11,000

Entry to record first interest payment:

Interest Expense ($111,000 x 6%)	6,660	
Notes Payable ($12,000 – $6,660)	5,340	
Cash ($100,000 x 12%)		12,000

Entry to record second interest payment:

Interest Expense		
($111,000 – $5,340) x 6%	6,340	
Notes Payable	5,660	
Cash		12,000

Entry to record principal payment at end of second year:

Notes Payable	100,000	
Cash		100,000

ILLUSTRATION: CASE 2

Assume the new terms are a reduction in principal to $80,000, payable in two years, with interest payable annually at 12%. The accrued interest is forgiven.

Future cash payments:

Interest: $80,000 x 12% x 2 years	$19,200
Principal payable in two years	80,000
Total	$99,200

Entry:

Interest Payable	11,000	
Notes Payable	800	
Gain on Debt Restructure		
($111,000 – $99,200)		11,800

No interest expense would be recognized in the future. The gain on restructure would be an extraordinary gain.

If a debt restructuring involves the transfer of an asset or issuance of equity securities to the creditor, the transaction is recorded on the basis of the fair market value of the asset or equity interest. Such market value would be less than the carrying value of the debt, since the creditor is granting a concession. The difference would be recognized as an extraordinary gain by the debtor. If an asset is transferred, the difference between the book value of the asset and its market value would be an ordinary gain or loss. Then the difference between the market value of the asset and the carrying value of the debt would be an extraordinary gain.

ILLUSTRATION

Assume the $111,000 debt in the previous illustration. The debtor issues 1,000 shares of its $50 par value common stock. The current market price of the stock is $75 per share.

Entry:

Notes Payable	100,000	
Interest Payable	11,000	
Common Stock (1,000 x $50)		50,000
Paid-in Capital in Excess of Par		
(1,000 x $25)		25,000
Gain on Restructuring of Debt		36,000

ILLUSTRATION

Assume the $111,000 debt in the previous illustration. The creditor agrees to accept as full settlement a piece of land owned by the debtor. The land cost $50,000, and has a current market value of $80,000.

Ordinary gain on disposal of property:
$80,000 - $50,000 = $30,000

Extraordinary gain on restructuring of debt:
$111,000 - $80,000 = $31,000

Entry:

Notes Payable	100,000	
Interest Payable	11,000	
Land		50,000
Gain on Disposal of Property		30,000
Gain on Restructuring of Debt		31,000

CHAPTER 11

STOCKHOLDERS' EQUITY

Equity is the residual interest in the assets of an entity. Thus, assets minus liabilities equals equity. In a business, this residual is the equity of the owners. The owners of a corporation are the **stockholders** and their interest in the assets of the corporation is called **stockholders' equity**.

Stockholders' equity consists of two components: **Paid-in capital**, equity resulting from contributions by the owners, and **retained earnings**, equity resulting from the operation of the business.

11.1 PAID-IN CAPITAL

A corporation is formed in the United States according to the laws of the state in which it is incorporated. The ownership of a corporation which is privately owned and organized for profit is divided into units called **shares** of **capital stock**. The types of stock and the number of shares authorized to be issued are stated in the **articles of incorporation**.

Common stock is the class of stock which represents the residual or basic ownership of the corporation. Owners of shares of common stock have an ownership interest in the corporation. Shares of common stock may be bought, sold, or otherwise transferred by stockholders, usually without the consent of the corporation. Ownership of shares generally confers the right to: (1) share in the management of the corporation, (2) share in the distribution of profits as dividends, (3) share in corporate assets upon liquidation, and (4) maintain the same ownership interest in the corporation by purchasing a proportionate number of any new shares which are issued (the preemptive right).

A corporation may also issue **preferred stock**. This class of stock usually grants its owners certain privileges in exchange for elimination of some of the rights previously mentioned.

Stockholders in corporations enjoy **limited liability**. They generally cannot be held liable for the debts of the corporation. In order to protect creditors of corporations, state laws generally provide for a **minimum legal capital**, the amount of stockholders' equity that cannot be distributed as dividends. Legal capital is usually determined by the **par value** or **stated value** of the shares of stock.

ISSUANCE OF STOCK

Stock may be issued in exchange for cash. To illustrate, assume the issuance of 1,000 shares of common stock which has a par value of $10 per share. The stock is issued for $15 per share. The entry to record the issuance would be:

Cash	15,000	
Common Stock, $10 Par		10,000
Paid-in Capital in Excess of Par		5,000

If the stock were no-par stock with a $10 stated value, the entry would be:

Cash	15,000	
Common Stock, $10 Stated Value		10,000
Paid-in Capital in Excess of Stated Value		5,000

If the stock were true no-par stock, with no stated value:

Cash	15,000	
Common Stock, No-Par		15,000

A corporation may choose to record authorized stock in the accounts. For example, assume the corporation in the above illustration was authorized at the time of incorporation to issue up to 10,000 shares of $10 par value common stock. At that time the following entry would be made:

Unissued Common Stock		
(10,000 x $10)	100,000	
Authorized Common Stock		100,000

When the 1,000 shares of stock are issued, the entry would be:

Cash	15,000	
Unissued Common Stock		10,000
Paid-in Capital in Excess of Par		5,000

The amount of issued stock at any time is determined as the balance of the authorized stock account minus the balance of the unissued stock account.

Stock may be sold on a subscription basis. A subscriber makes some initial partial payment and makes additional payments until the full price is paid. The stock is not issued until the full subscription price is paid.

To illustrate, assume subscriptions are received for 1,000 shares of the $10 par value common stock at a selling price of $15 per share. An initial payment of $3,750 is received on the subscriptions. The balance is payable in three equal installments. The entry for the initial payment would be:

Cash	3,750	
Subscriptions Receivable,		
Common Stock	11,250	
Common Stock Subscribed		
(1,000 x $10 par)		10,000
Additional Paid-in Capital		
on Common Stock		5,000

The Common Stock Subscribed account should be reported as part of Paid-in Capital in Stockholders' Equity. There is disagreement about the proper reporting of the Subscriptions Receivable account balance. Some believe it is an asset just as other receivables. Others believe it should be reported as contra (negative) stockholders' equity.

The entry for the collection of the last installment on the subscriptions and the issuance of stock would be:

Cash	3,750	
Subscriptions Receivable,		
Common Stock		3,750
Common Stock Subscribed	10,000	
Common Stock, $10 Par		10,000

If a subscriber fails to complete payment, the disposition of the amount paid and the unpaid balance will depend largely on the state law. Possibilities include refund of amounts paid, issuance of the number of shares covered by the partial payment, or forfeiture of all payments to the corporation.

Stock may be issued in exchange for noncash assets or services. The general principle is that the issue price of the stock, and thus the basis for accounting, is the fair market value of the assets or services or the fair market value of the stock issued, whichever is more clearly determinable.

For example, assume that 1,000 shares of $10 par value common stock are issued in exchange for a piece of land. An appraisal indicates that the current fair market value of the land is $14,000. The entry to record the stock issuance would be:

Land	14,000	
Common Stock, $10 Par		10,000
Paid-in Capital in Excess of Par		4,000

A corporation may incur significant costs in connection with the issuance of stock. Examples are registration fees, underwriting commissions, legal and accounting fees, and printing costs. Two methods of accounting for these **stock issue costs** are used. These costs may be considered as a reduction of the amount received for the issuance of the stock or as an intangible asset and amortized over a reasonable period of time, not to exceed 40 years.

PREFERRED STOCK

Preferred stock grants certain preferences to its owners as compared to common stock. These preferences typically relate to dividends and assets in liquidation. Preferred stock may also be convertible into

127

other securities or be callable or redeemable. Accounting for the issuance of preferred stock generally parallels that for common stock.

Preferred stock usually grants a preference as to dividends. If the stock is par value, the preference is stated as a percentage. For example, 6% preferred stock grants a preference of 6% of par value. That is, if the corporation declares any dividends, the preferred stockholders must get the 6% dividend before common stockholders receive dividends.

To illustrate, assume the following stock outstanding:

6% preferred stock, $100 par value,	
10,000 shares authorized and issued	$1,000,000
Common stock, $10 par value,	
500,000 shares authorized,	
200,000 issued	2,000,000
Total	$3,000,000

The corporation declares a total dividend of $150,000:

Dividend to preferred (6% x $1,000,000)	$ 60,000
Balance to common	90,000
Total	$ 150,000

Preferred stock may be **cumulative** or **noncumulative** as to dividends. If cumulative, any dividends to preferred which are not paid become **dividends in arrears** which must be paid before any dividends can be paid to common. If the stock is noncumulative, any dividends passed in prior years are lost by the stockholders. Most preferred stock is cumulative.

To illustrate, assume the stock outstanding in the previous example.

Dividends in arrears:	19x1	$ 60,000
	19x2	60,000

In 19x3, the corporation pays total dividends of $250,000:

Payable to preferred:	
19x1 and 19x2 dividends in arrears	$120,000
19x3 dividend	60,000
Total	$180,000

Payable to common:	
($250,000 – $180,000)	$ 70,000

In addition, preferred stock may be **fully participating, partially participating**, or **nonparticipating**. If fully participating, the stock participates in any dividends paid above its preferred rate. For example, if the 6% preferred in the above example is fully participating, it would receive its 6% preference and, after common stock has received 6%, would receive a pro rata share of any additional dividends. If the stock were partially participating, some upper limit on dividends on the preferred would be set. For example, the stock may be participating up to 10%, meaning that it would participate pro rata in dividends above 6% to maximum dividend to preferred of 10%. If the preferred were nonparticipating, its annual dividend would be limited to its 6% preference.

EXAMPLE

Assume the preferred stock in the above examples is cumulative and fully participating. The 19x1 preferred dividend is in arrears. The total 19x2 dividend is $300,000.

	Preferred	Common
Dividend in arrears		
(6% x $1,000,000)	$60,000	
19x2 dividend to preferred (6%)	60,000	
Matching 6% to common		
(6% x $2,000,000)		$120,000
Balance shared pro rata*	20,000	40,000
Total	$140,000	$160,000

*Shared pro rata according to par value outstanding:

Preferred	$1,000,000	(1/3)
Common	2,000,000	(2/3)
Total	$3,000,000	

TREASURY STOCK

Stock which a corporation has issued and then reacquired is called **treasury stock**. Such reacquired stock is not an asset, since a corporation cannot own itself. There are two generally used methods of

129

accounting for treasury stock, the **cost method** and the **par (or stated) value method.**

In the cost method, the purchase of treasury stock is recorded with a debit to Treasury Stock for the cost of the shares. This account is a contra account in stockholders' equity. When the stock is reissued, the account is credited for the cost of the shares sold. If the shares are sold for more than their cost, the excess is credited to an equity account, Paid-in Capital, from Treasury Stock Transactions. If the stock is sold for less than its cost, the difference is debited to Paid-in Capital from Treasury Stock Transactions. If that account does not have a balance large enough to absorb all of the difference, the excess is debited to Retained Earnings.

EXAMPLE

A corporation purchases 1,000 shares of its common stock on the open market for $12 per share.

Treasury Stock, Common (1,000 x $12)	12,000	
Cash		12,000

500 of the treasury shares are sold for $14 per share:

Cash (500 x $14)	7,000	
Treasury Stock, Common (500 x $12)		6,000
Paid-in Capital from Treasury Stock Transactions		1,000

Later, the remaining 500 shares are sold for $11 per share.

Cash (500 x $11)	5,500	
Paid-in Capital from Treasury Stock Transactions	500	
Treasury Stock, Common (500 x $12)		6,000

The par value method views the acquisition of the treasury stock as essentially a retirement of the stock and the reissuance as a new issue. At acquisition, Treasury Stock is debited for the par value (or stated value or average issue price for no par stock) of the shares acquired. Any paid-in capital in excess of par related to the stock is eliminated. If the treasury stock is acquired at a cost greater than the original issue price of the stock, the excess is debited to Paid-in Capital from Treasury Stock Transactions to the extent available, with any additional amount debited to Retained Earnings. If the stock is acquired for less than original issue price, the difference is credited to Paid-in Capital from Treasury Stock Transactions. When the treasury stock is reissued, the accounting follows that for new issues of stock.

EXAMPLE

Using the data from the cost method illustration above, assume that the stock has a par value of $10 per share and was originally issued for $15 per share.

Acquisition:

Treasury Stock, Common		
(1,000 x $10)	10,000	
Paid-in Capital in Excess of Par	5,000	
Cash		12,000
Paid-in Capital from Treasury		
Stock Transactions		3,000

Reissue of 500 shares at $14 per share:

Cash (500 x $14)	7,000	
Treasury Stock, Common		
(500 x $10)		5,000
Paid-in Capital in Excess of Par		2,000

Reissue of 500 shares at $11 per share:

Cash (500 x $11)	5,500	
Treasury Stock, Common		
(500 x $10)		5,000
Paid-in Capital in Excess of Par		500

EXAMPLE

Assume that the treasury stock acquisition cost was $18 per share and that there was a $2,000 previous balance in Paid-in Capital from Treasury Stock Transactions:

Acquisition:

Treasury Stock, Common		
(1,000 x $10 par)	10,000	
Paid-in Capital in Excess of Par	5,000	
Paid-in Capital from Treasury		

Stock Transactions	2,000	
Retained Earnings	1,000	
Cash		18,000

If the cost method is used, the balance sheet would report the balance of the Treasury Stock account as a deduction from total paid-in capital and retained earnings to arrive at total stockholders' equity. Under the par value method, the Treasury Stock account balance (at par) is deducted from the related stock account balance in paid-in capital.

CALLABLE AND REDEEMABLE STOCK

Preferred stock issues sometimes contain a **call provision**, allowing the corporation to reacquire, at its option, shares of the stock at a specified price. **Redeemable** preferred stock, on the other hand, gives the stockholder the option to return the stock to the corporation at a specified price. If such stock is called or redeemed, the original issue amounts of paid-in capital should be debited. If the call or redemption price is greater than the original issue price, the excess is debited to Retained Earnings. If the call or redemption price is less than the original issue price, the difference is credited to a paid-in capital account such as Paid-in Capital from Retirement of Stock.

EXAMPLE

Assume 10,000 shares outstanding of $100 par value preferred stock, originally issued at $105 per share and callable at $110 per share. All of the preferred shares are called.

Preferred Stock (10,000 x $100)	1,000,000	
Paid-in Capital in Excess of Par, Preferred Stock	50,000	
Retained Earnings	50,000	
Cash (10,000 x $110)		1,100,000

CONVERTIBLE STOCK

Preferred stock may be issued which gives the stockholder the option, under specified conditions, to convert the preferred stock into some other type of stock, usually common, at a stated exchange rate.

EXAMPLE

Assume 10,000 shares outstanding of $100 par value preferred stock, each share convertible into 8 shares of $10 par value common. The preferred was originally issued at $105 per share. 1,000 shares of the preferred is converted.

Preferred Stock (1,000 x $100)	100,000	
Paid-in Capital in Excess of Par,		
Preferred Stock	5,000	
Common Stock (8,000 x $10)		80,000
Paid-in Capital in Excess of Par,		
Common Stock		
($105,000 – $80,000)		25,000

If the par value of the common stock in the example above were greater than the issue price of the preferred, the difference would be debited to Retained Earnings.

STOCK RIGHTS AND OPTIONS

Stock rights or **options** grant the holder the right to acquire stock in a corporation under specified terms. The certificate documenting such rights is called a **stock warrant.**

A corporation may issue stock rights to existing shareholders in connection with a new issue of stock as evidence of the preemptive right. No entry, other than a possible memorandum, is made when the rights are issued. When rights are exercised, the issuance of stock is recorded as for any new stock issue.

A corporation may issue stock rights to improve the marketability of other securities such as bonds or preferred stock. If the rights are in the form of detachable stock warrants, the issue price of the securities must be allocated between the bonds or preferred stock and the warrants on the basis of their relative market value.

EXAMPLE

A corporation issues 1,000 shares of $100 par value preferred stock. Each share includes one detachable stock warrant. Each warrant grants the right to purchase one share of $10 par value common stock at $20 per share. The issue price of the preferred is $106 per share. The market value of the preferred stock without the warrants is $104 per share. The market value of the warrants is $5 each.

Allocation of issue price:

$$\frac{\text{Market Value of warrants}}{\text{Market value of warrants and stock}} \times \$106,000 = \text{Issue price of Warrants}$$

$$\frac{\text{Market Value of stock}}{\text{Market value of warrants and stock}} \times \$106,000 = \text{Issue price of Stock}$$

$$\frac{1,000 \times \$5}{(1,000 \times \$5) + (1,000 \times \$104)} = \frac{\$5,000}{\$109,000} \times \$106,000 =$$

$$= \$4,862.38 = \text{Issue price of warrants}$$

$$\frac{1,000 \times \$5}{(1,000 \times \$5) + (1,000 \times \$104)} = \frac{\$5,000}{\$109,000} \times \$106,000 =$$

$$= \$101,137.62 = \text{Issue price of stock}$$

The entry to record the issue of the stock:

Cash (1,000 x $106)	106,000	
Preferred Stock (1,000 x $100 par)		100,000
Paid-in Capital in Excess of Par, Preferred Stock ($101,138 − $100,000)		1,138
Common Stock Warrants		4,862

Assume that one-half of the outstanding warrants are exercised.

Cash (500 x $20)	10,000	
Common Stock Warrants (1/2 x $4,862)	2,431	
Common Stock (500 x $10 par)		5,000
Paid-in Capital in Excess of Par, Common Stock		7,431

Assume that the remaining warrants expire.

Common Stock Warrants	2,431	
Paid-in Capital from		
Expired Warrants		2,431

A corporation may issue stock options as compensation to employees, particularly officers and other key employees. The compensation cost is the difference between the market price of the related stock and the option price on the **measurement date**. The measurement date is the date on which are known **both** the number of shares a person is entitled to receive and the purchase price, if any. This compensation cost should be allocated as expense to those periods in which the company receives the benefit from the employee's services.

EXAMPLE

The measurement date is the date of the grant of the options. An option is granted to an officer to purchase 1,000 shares of $10 par common stock at $20 per share. On the date of the grant the market price is $30 per share. The period of service to which this compensation applies is the following five years.

Grant of the options:

Deferred Compensation Expense		
[1,000 x ($30 – $20)]	10,000	
Stock Options Outstanding		10,000

Recognition of expense, each of the next five years:

Compensation Expense		
(1/5 x $10,000)	2,000	
Deferred Compensation Expense		2,000

Assume the option is exercised at the end of the five years:

Cash (1,000 x $20)	20,000	
Stock Options Outstanding	10,000	
Common Stock (1,000 x $10)		10,000
Paid-in Capital in Excess of Par,		
Common Stock		20,000

The account Stock Options Outstanding is a paid-in capital account and Deferred Compensation Expense is contra to it, with its balance deducted from Stock Options Outstanding in the paid-in capital section of stockholders' equity on the balance sheet.

If the measurement date is after the date of the grant, compensation expense must be estimated until the measurement date is reached.

STOCK APPRECIATION RIGHTS

Stock appreciation rights give employees the right to receive cash based on the difference between the grant price and the market price of the company's stock on the exercise date. This difference represents compensation expense which should be allocated to the periods of service in which the compensation is earned. The exact amount of the compensation is not likely to be known until the exercise date. Therefore, if the period of service precedes that date, the expense must be estimated. These estimates result in a **liability** since cash payments are expected in the future.

11.2 RETAINED EARNINGS

Retained earnings is the stockholders' equity amount which represents the equity resulting from the operations of the business. More specifically, the retained earnings balance is the accumulated net income of the entity minus net losses and dividends, plus or minus prior period adjustments. A debit balance in retained earnings is called a **deficit**.

DIVIDENDS

Dividends are distributions of a corporation's earnings to its stockholders through a transfer of assets or stock. Such distributions result in a decrease in Retained Earnings and a decrease in assets or an increase in capital stock accounts.

Dividends are declared by the corporation's board of directors. The **declaration date** is the date on which the board declares the dividend. It is payable to stockholders who are recorded as owners on the **date of record**, a date specified by the board and usually a few weeks after the declaration date. An **ex-dividend date** is usually specified as a few days before the record date to allow time to record all transfers of stock by the record date. Investors acquiring the stock on or after the ex-dividend date will not receive the dividend. The dividend is paid on a specified **date of payment.**

Dividends usually are distributed as cash. To illustrate the accounting for a cash dividend, assume the board of directors declared a 25 cents per share dividend on its 100,000 outstanding shares of common stock. The dividend was declared on April 1, 19x1, payable on June 1 to stockholders of record on May 10.

Entry on April 1 (date of declaration):

Retained Earnings (100,000 x $.25)	25,000	
Cash Dividends Payable		25,000

No accounting entry is required on May 10 (date of record).

Entry on June 1 (date of payment):

Cash Dividends Payable	25,000	
Cash		25,000

A corporation may distribute a dividend in the form of noncash assets, a **property dividend.** For example, the company may distribute to its stockholders shares of stock in another corporation which have been held as an investment. Such a distribution is considered a nonmonetary transaction and, specifically, a nonreciprocal transfer. Such a transaction must be accounted for on the basis of the current market value of the assets transferred.

EXAMPLE

Assume a corporation owns 1,000 shares of stock of XYZ, Inc. This stock was acquired at a cost of $20,000. The board of directors declared a dividend which will result in the distribution of the XYZ stock to common stockholders. The current market value of the XYZ stock is $30,000.

On date of declaration:

Investment in XYZ, Inc. Stock		
($30,000 – $20,000)	10,000	
Gain on Disposal of Investment		10,000
Retained Earnings	30,000	
Property Dividend Payable		30,000

On date of payment:

137

| Property Dividend Payable | 30,000 | |
| Investment in XYZ, Inc. Stock | | 30,000 |

If a corporation declares a dividend in an amount in excess of the balance of Retained Earnings, the excess is a **liquidating dividend**, a return to stockholders of amounts they paid in. The excess should be debited to paid-in capital, rather than retained earnings. Full disclosure should be made to stockholders of the nature of the dividend.

A corporation may declare a dividend payable at a later date and issue notes ("scrip") to the stockholders. Such a **scrip dividend** is recorded with a credit to Notes Payable to Stockholders on the date of declaration. At the maturity of the notes, this account is debited, along with Interest Expense, if necessary.

A corporation may declare a **stock dividend,** distributing proportionately to its stockholders additional shares of the same stock already owned. Such a dividend does not change a stockholder's percentage of ownership in the corporation and is not considered income. The general rule in accounting is that for a relatively small stock dividend (less than 20-25% of the shares outstanding), retained earnings should be debited for the market value of the additional shares issued. Paid-in capital is credited, thus changing the components but not the total of stockholders' equity. For a larger stock dividend, the debit to retained earnings should be for only such amount as required to satisfy the legal capital requirements of state law. Thus a large stock dividend should result in a debit to retained earnings of the amount of the total par or stated value of the shares to be distributed.

EXAMPLE

Assume a corporation with 100,000 shares of $10 par value common stock outstanding declares a 10% stock dividend. On the date of declaration, the market value of the stock is $15 per share.

Date of Declaration:

Retained Earnings		
(10% x 100,000 x $15)	150,000	
Common Stock Dividend Distributable		
(10,000 shares x $10 par)		100,000
Paid-in Capital in Excess of Par		50,000

Date of Distribution:

| Common Stock Dividend Distributable | 100,000 | |
| Common Stock, $10 Par | | 100,000 |

EXAMPLE

Assume that the dividend above was 50%:

Date of Declaration:

Retained Earnings		
(50% x 100,000 x $10 par)	500,000	
Common Stock Dividend Distributable		500,000

Date of Distribution:

| Common Stock Dividend Distributable | 500,000 | |
| Common Stock, $10 Par | | 500,000 |

STOCK SPLITS

A corporation may wish to reduce the market value per share of its stock and therefore uses a **stock split**. In a split, the par or stated value of the shares is reduced and the number of shares outstanding is proportionately increased. For example, if a corporation had outstanding 100,000 shares of $10 par value stock, a 2 for 1 stock split would mean the par value would be reduced to $5 per share and the number of shares increased to 200,000. The split does not affect the total stockholders' equity nor the total paid-in capital. No entry is required except perhaps a memorandum to record the new par value and number of shares outstanding. In a **reverse stock split**, the par or stated value is increased and the number of shares correspondingly decreased.

APPROPRIATIONS OF RETAINED EARNINGS

A corporation's board of directors may decide to reclassify a portion of Retained Earnings as restricted, or **appropriated**, to formally recognize that some of the corporation's assets are being withheld from dividend distribution. Such restrictions on dividends may be related to legal or contractual requirements or be from a board decision to retain assets for future use by the corporation. When such an appropriation is made, retained earnings is debited and an appropriately titled appropriated retained earnings account is credited. When the appropriation is determined to be no longer necessary, the appropriated retained earnings is returned to unappropriated status with a debit to appropriated retained earnings and a credit to retained earnings.

139

CHAPTER 12

LEASES

A **lease** is a contractual agreement in which a **lessor**, owner of property such as equipment, machinery, or vehicles, grants to the **lessee** the use of the property for a period of time in return for periodic cash payments (rent) by the lessee to the lessor. Accounting for leases has been complicated by the fact that, in many cases, what is called a lease is in substance an installment sale and purchase of the "leased" asset.

The FASB established in **SFAS 13** the general principle that "a lease that transfers substantially all of the benefits and risks incident to ownership of property should be accounted for as the acquisition of an asset and the incurrence of an obligation by the lessee and as a sale or financing by the lessor." Other leases which do not fit this description are accounted for as "true" leases or rentals of the property. Implementation of these general principles is described in the remainder of this chapter.

12.1 CLASSIFICATION OF LEASES

SFAS 13 identifies four criteria for classification of leases. If any **one** of these criteria is met by a particular lease, the lease is to be classified and accounted for as a **capital lease** by the lessee. If none of these criteria is met, the lease is an **operating lease**. If one of the four criteria is met and two additional criteria are met by a particular lease, the lease is a capital lease for the lessor. Otherwise it is an operating lease.

The four criteria are:

1. The lease transfers ownership of the property to the lessee by the end of the lease term.

2. The lease contains a **bargain purchase option** (giving the lessee the option to purchase the leased property for a price sufficiently low that exercise of the option appears to be reasonably assured).

3. The lease term is equal to 75% or more of the estimated economic life of the leased property.

4. The present value at the beginning of the lease term of the minimum lease payments, excluding executory costs, equals or exceeds 90% of the fair value of the leased property. The interest rate to be used in calculating the present value is the lessee's incremental borrowing rate or the implicit rate computed by the lessor, if known to the lessee and lower than the incremental rate. Executory costs are expenses such as insurance and maintenance normally incurred during the useful life of leased assets.

If any one of the above four criteria is met for a particular lease, it should be accounted for as a capital lease by the lessee. Otherwise, it is an operating lease.

For the lessor, if any one of the four criteria is met and two other conditions are met, the lease is a **direct financing** or **sales-type** lease. Otherwise, it is an operating lease. The two additional criteria are:

1. Collectability of the minimum lease payments is reasonably predictable.

2. No important uncertainties surround the amount of unreimbursable costs yet to be incurred by the lessor under the lease.

12.2 ACCOUNTING BY LESSEES

A lessee accounts for a capital lease by recognizing an asset (the leased property) and a liability (the lease payment obligation). The amount recognized is the lesser of (1) the present value at inception of the lease of the minimum lease payments, and (2) the fair value of the leased property at inception of the lease. The asset is amortized (depreciated) and the periodic lease payments reduce the balance of the liability.

EXAMPLE

On January 1, 19x1, a lease is initiated for equipment. The lease covers a period of five years and is noncancelable. Payments of $23,982 are payable at the beginning of each year (first payment due 1/1/x1). All executory costs are payable separately by the lessee. The current market value of the leased asset is $100,000. The lessee's incremental borrowing rate is 10%. The lessor's interest rate implicit in the lease is also 10%, and this rate is known to the lessee. The estimated useful life of the leased asset is five years. There is no bargain purchase option. Title to the leased asset remains with the lessor. The estimated residual value of the asset at the end of the five years is zero.

Is this a capital lease to the lessee?

Test it against the four criteria:

1. Ownership is **not** transferred to the lessee. This criterion is **not** met.

2. There is **no** bargain purchase option. This criterion is **not** met.

3. The lease term is 100% of the estimated economic life of the property. This criterion **is** met.

4. The present value of the minimum lease payments:

PV of annuity due of $23,982, 5 payments,
discounted at 10% = $23,984 x 4.16987 = $100,000
(approx.).

Thus the present value equals 100% of the fair value of the leased property. This criterion **is** met.

Since at least one of the four criteria is met, the lease is a capital lease to the lessee.

Entry to record lease:

Leased Equipment	100,000	
Leased Obligation		100,000

The periodic lease payments should be allocated as interest expense and reduction of principal accomplished by the effective interest method.

(1)	(2)	(3)	(4)	(5)
	Annual			**Balance**
	Lease	**Interest**	**Principal**	**of Lease**
Date	**Payment**	**10% x col. 5**	**(2) – (3)**	**Obligation**
Jan. 1, 19x1	Inception			$100,000
Jan. 1, 19x1	$23,982	$ -0-	$ 23,982	76,018
Jan. 1, 19x2	23,982	7,602	16,380	59,638
Jan. 1, 19x3	23,982	5,964	18,018	41,620
Jan. 1, 19x4	23,982	4,162	19,820	21,800
Jan. 1, 19x5	23,982	2,182*	21,800	-0-

*Adjusted for effects of rounding.

The entry of the January 1, 19x1, lease payment:

Lease Obligation	23,982	
Cash		23,982

Adjusting entry on December 31, 19x1, to accrue interest:

Interest Expense	7,602	
Interest Payable		7,602

Entry for January 1, 19x2, payment, assuming reversing entries are not made:

Lease Obligation	16,380	
Interest Payable	7,602	
Cash		23,982

If title to the property passes to the lessee or there is a bargain purchase option, the cost of the leased asset should be depreciated over the asset's useful life. Otherwise, the cost should be amortized over the term of the lease. In this example, therefore, amortization should be over five years — the term of the lease (which is the same as the useful life in this case).

Assuming straight line depreciation, the annual entry would be:

Depreciation Expense, Leased Equipment	20,000	
Accumulated Depreciation, Leased Equipment		20,000

At the expiration of the lease the equipment would be returned to the lessor. The lease obligation would have been fully paid. The leased asset and related accumulated depreciation would be removed from the accounts:

Accumulated Depreciation,		
Leased Equipment	100,000	
Leased Equipment		100,000

Expenses for maintenance, insurance, taxes, and other executory costs would be recognized as incurred over the five years.

If none of the four criteria is met by a lease, it is an operating lease to the lessee. The only entries required would be for the annual payments, which would be recorded as rent expense.

EXAMPLE

On January 1, 19x1, a lease is initiated for equipment. The lease covers a period of three years. Payments of $25,000 are payable at the beginning of each year (first payment 1/1/x1). The current market value of the leased asset is $100,000. The lessee's incremental borrowing rate is 10%. The lessor's interest rate implicit in the lease is also 10%, and this rate is known to the lessee. The estimated useful life of the leased equipment is five years. There is no bargain purchase option. Title to the leased asset remains with the lessor.

Test the four criteria:

1.   Title is not transferred to the lessee.

2.   There is no bargain purchase option.

3.   The lease term is 60% of the estimated economic life of the asset.

4.   The present value of the minimum lease payments:

Present value of annuity due of $25,000, 3 payments, at 10% = $25,000 x 2.73554 = $68,388.50

The present value is 68.4% ($68,388.50 / $100,000) of the fair value of the asset.

None of the four criteria is met. Therefore, the lease is an operating lease.

The entry for each payment would be:

Rent Expense	25,000	
Cash		25,000

12.3 ACCOUNTING BY LESSORS

If a lease does not meet any of the four criteria, or if it meets one or more of these criteria but does not meet both of the additional conditions described above, the lease is an operating lease to the lessor. The lessor would record the lease payments as rental revenue earned and would recognize depreciation expense on the leased property over the asset's useful life.

If a lease does meet one or more of the four criteria and the other two conditions, it is either a direct financing lease or a sales-type lease to the lessor. It is a direct financing lease if the asset's fair value is equal to the asset's book value to the lessor. It is a sales-type lease if the fair value is greater than the book value, thus involving a markup.

In a direct financing lease the lease payments are calculated to recover the book value (cost to lessor) of the leased asset plus interest at the market rate. The only revenue recognized by the lessor is the interest on the lease. The total amount of interest is the difference between the asset's book value (which equals the market value) and the gross investment in the lease. The gross investment is the sum of the minimum lease payments plus any unguaranteed residual value of the asset to the lessor.

EXAMPLE

On January 1, 19x1, a lessor leases a piece of equipment for a period of 5 years. Annual payments of $23,892 are payable at the beginning of each year (first payment due 1/1/x1). The cost of the equipment to the lessor and its current fair market value are $100,000. The lease payments are calculated to provide interest at 10%. The estimated useful life of the asset is 5 years. There is no bargain purchase option. Title to the leased asset remains with the lessor. The estimated residual value of the asset at the end of the five years is zero. Collectability of the minimum lease payments is reasonably assured and no important uncertainties surround the lease concerning costs yet to be incurred by the lessor under the lease.

Since the lease term is 100% of the equipment's useful life and the present value of the minimum lease payments is more than 90% of the fair value of the property (see previous illustration for calculation) and the two additional conditions are met, the lease is a capital lease to the lessor. Since the cost of the equipment is equal to its current fair value, the lease is a direct financing lease.

Gross investment in lease   = minimum lease payments
                                + residual value
                              = ($23,982 x 5) + 0 = $119,910

Total interest   = Gross investment – fair
                                market value
                              = $119,910 – $100,000 = $19,910

Entry to record initiation of the lease:

Lease Receivable	119,910	
Equipment (cost)		100,000
Unearned Interest on Leases		19,910

Entry to record lease payment received on 1/1/x1:

Cash	23,982	
Lease Receivable		23,982

Entry to accrue interest on 12/31/x1 (amounts based on amortization schedule in previous illustration):

Unearned Interest on Leases	7,602	
Interest Revenue – Leases		7,602

Entry to record receipt of second lease payment on 1/1/x2:

Cash	23,982	
Lease Receivable		23,982

The preceding entries are based on use of the gross method of accounting for the receivable. As an alternative, the net method may be used:

To record the lease:

Lease Receivable	100,000	
Asset (cost)		100,000

First lease payment (1/1/x1):

Cash	23,982	
Lease Receivable		23,982

To accrue interest on 12/31/x1:

Interest Receivable – Leases	7,602	
Interest Revenue – Leases		7,602

Receipt of second lease payment 1/1/x2, assuming reversing entry not made:

Cash	23,982	
Interest Receivable – Leases		7,602
Lease Receivable		16,380

A lease is a sales-type lease to the lessor if the criteria for capital leases are met and the book value (or cost) of the leased asset is different from (usually less than) the fair value of the asset at the inception of the lease. In a sales-type lease the lessor recognizes profit on the sale of the asset as well as interest.

Fair value of asset – book value = Gross profit on sale

Gross investment in lease – fair value = Interest

EXAMPLE

Assume the same basic information as in the direct financing lease example above, but the book value of the equipment to the lessor is $90,000.

Gross profit on sale = $100,000 – $90,000 = $10,000

Interest = $119,910 – $100,000 = $19,910

Entry at inception of lease (assuming use of net method):

Lease Receivable	100,000	
Cost of Goods Sold	90,000	
Sales Revenue		100,000
Asset (cost)		90,000

Entries for collection of lease payments and accrual of interest would be the same as for the direct financing lease example.

12.4 OTHER ISSUES IN ACCOUNTING FOR LEASES

RESIDUAL VALUE

A leased asset may have a residual value at the end of the lease term. A lease agreement may require the lessee to guarantee a specified residual value to the lessor. Such **guaranteed residual value** is included as part of the minimum lease payments and thus as part of the lease receivable to the lessor and the lease payable to the lessee. The guaranteed residual value may not be the same as the expected residual value. The lessee should calculate depreciation on the basis of the expected residual value.

An **unguaranteed residual value** is included by a lessor in the gross investment in the lease. Its present value is included in the net investment in the lease and deducted in arriving at the amount to be recovered through the lease payments.

EXAMPLE

Equipment which cost a lessor $200,000 is leased for five years on a direct financing lease. The equipment is expected to have a residual value, unguaranteed, of $25,000 at the end of the lease. The lessor retains title to the equipment. The lessor seeks a return of 10% on the lease.

Cost of equipment	$200,000
Less: Present value at 10% of residual value = .68301 x $25,000	17,075
Amount to be recovered through lease payments	$182,925
Annual lease payment required, assuming first payment at beginning of lease (annuity due) = $182,925/4.16987	$43,868.27

At the end of the term of the lease, the lease receivable account balance should be $25,000. The equipment would be returned to the lessor.

Entry at end of lease:

Equipment	25,000	
Lease Receivable		25,000

INITIAL DIRECT COSTS

A lessor may incur some costs in negotiating and finalizing a lease. Examples are legal fees and sales commissions. For an operating lease, these **initial direct costs** are capitalized and amortized as expense as the rental revenue is recognized. For a sales-type lease, these costs are charged as part of the cost of sales in the year the lease (sale) is recorded. For a direct financing lease, these costs are added to the net investment in the lease and the effective interest rate adjusted to that rate, which equates the present value of the minimum lease payments plus any unguaranteed residual value to the revised net investment.

SALE-LEASEBACK

A **sale-leaseback** is a transaction in which an owner of property (seller-lessee) sells the property and immediately leases it back from the new owner (buyer-lessor). If the seller-lessee retains substantially all the rights to use the property, no gain should be recognized on the sale. If the leaseback qualifies as a capital lease, any gain on the sale should be deferred and amortized as a credit to depreciation expense or revenue over the same term as the leased property is depreciated or amortized. If the leaseback is an operating lease, any gain is deferred and amortized in proportion to the rental expense recognized over the term of the lease.

EXAMPLE

On January 1, 19x1, a company sold the building housing its offices for $800,000. The building had a book value of $750,000 on that date. The company immediately leased the building back for a period of 20 years with annual lease payments of $85,425, the first payment due on 1/1/x1. The lease qualifies as a capital lease to the seller-lessee. The lessor's implicit rate is 10%, the same as the lessee's incremental borrowing rate.

Entry for sale of building:

Cash	800,000	
Buildings		750,000
Unearned Profit on Sale-Leaseback		50,000

Entry to record leaseback as capital lease:

Leased Building	800,000	
Lease Obligation		800,000

149

Entry to record first lease payment, 1/1/x1:

Lease Obligation	85,425	
Cash		85,425

Entry to accrue interest on 12/31/x1:

Interest Expense		
[10% x ($800,000 – $85,425)]	71,458	
Interest Payable		71,458

Entry to record depreciation on building, assuming straight-line:

Depreciation Expense		
($800,000 / 20)	40,000	
Accumulated Depreciation		40,000

Entry to record amortization of unrecognized gain:

Unearned Profit on Sale-Leaseback		
($50,000 /20)	2,500	
Depreciation Expense		2,500

Other rules apply in accounting for sale-leasebacks in cases where the seller-lessee retains only a minor part of the rights of use of the property or more than a minor part but less than substantially all. Other rules also apply for sales and leasebacks of real estate.

CHAPTER 13

PENSIONS

Many employers provide pension or retirement benefits for their employees. As a general principle, the cost of providing the pension benefits earned by employees during a period in which the employees render services should be recognized as compensation expense in that period. To the extent that an employer has not contributed assets sufficient to fund the benefits earned to date by employees, the shortfall is a liability to the employer. The accounting issues relating to pensions center around the measurement and reporting of this pension cost and liability.

13.1 THE NATURE OF PENSION PLANS

Pension plans are broadly classified into two types. A **defined contribution plan** requires the employer to make specified contributions into a pension plan. The benefits a particular employee will receive upon retirement are based on the contributions made and the investment earnings of the plan. A **defined benefit plan** promises a specified benefit to retirees. The annual pension cost and required contributions to the plan are based on estimates of the cost of providing the stipulated benefits.

Accounting for defined contribution plans is relatively straightforward. The annual pension cost equals the contribution required by the provisions of the plan. A pension liability would be reported to the extent the required contribution has not been made by the employer.

Accounting for defined benefit plans is much more complex. Measurement of the annual pension cost and required contribution depends on estimates of the effects of a number of variables, such as future salary levels, longevity of retirees, and investment earnings rate. Projections of the pension cost are made by specialists called **actuaries**. The accountant's role is the proper accounting and reporting for the pension cost and related liability.

Accounting by employers for pensions is governed by **SFAS 87**. This standard outlines the procedure for measuring and reporting pension expense and pension liability, including an additional minimum liability. The remainder of this chapter deals with the accounting for defined benefit plans as required by **SFAS 87**.

A few important definitions of pension terms are given below to facilitate the discussion that follows.

Accumulated benefit obligation—actuarial present value of benefits attributed by the pension benefit formula to employee service rendered before a specified date and based on employee service and compensation prior to that date. No assumption is made about future compensation levels.

Net periodic pension cost—the amount recognized in an employer's financial statements as the cost of a pension plan for a period.

Plan assets—assets – usually stocks, bonds, and other investments – that have been segregated and restricted (usually in a trust) to provide benefits.

Projected benefit obligation—the actuarial present value, as of a date of all benefits attributed by the pension benefit formula to employee service rendered prior to that date. The projected benefit obligation is measured using assumptions as to future compensation levels if the pension benefit formula is based on those future compensation levels.

Prior service cost—the cost of retroactive benefits granted in a plan amendment.

13.2 BASIC PRINCIPLES OF ACCOUNTING FOR PENSIONS

Accounting for pension activities such as receipt and investment of pension contributions and payment of benefits to retirees is done outside the general ledger accounting records of the employer company. The employer's financial statements reflect pension cost on the income statement and prepaid or accrued pension cost on the balance sheet based on information from the activities of the pension plan.

Two events are involved in the general ledger accounting for pensions. First is the measurement of net periodic pension cost. Second is the funding of the pension obligation. The measurement of pension cost is done using information from the pension plan's actuaries and other sources. The measurement of pension cost is on the basis of the **projected benefit obligation** if the pension plan provides for benefits based on future compensation levels. The funding decision is made by management based on various factors, such as financial management and income tax considerations.

The accounting for pension cost involves a debit to Pension Expense and a credit to Prepaid/Accrued Pension Cost. The accounting for funding involves a debit to Prepaid/Accrued Pension Cost and a credit to Cash. If, after these entries, the Prepaid/Accrued Pension Cost has a net debit balance, it is reported as an asset. If the account has a net credit balance, it is reported as a liability.

EXAMPLE

Assume an employer's pension cost for the current year is determined to be $300,000. Management decides that it can only fund $250,000.

Pension Expense	300,000	
Prepaid/Accrued Pension Cost		300,000
Prepaid/Accrued Pension Cost	250,000	
Cash		250,000

These two entries could be combined into one:

Pension Expense	300,000	
Cash		250,000
Prepaid/Accrued Pension Cost		50,000

153

The credit balance in Prepaid/Accrued Pension Cost would be reported as a liability.

The FASB standard requires recognition of a **minimum liability** for pensions for any period to the extent that the **accumulated benefit obligation** exceeds the fair value of the pension plan assets at year-end. If this minimum liability is greater than any existing credit balance in Prepaid/Accrued Pension Cost, an additional liability must be recognized. If there is a debit balance in Prepaid/Accrued Pension Cost, the additional liability adjustment will be for the minimum liability plus the debit balance. For reporting purposes, the debit balance is netted against the additional liability. The account debited in recognizing the additional liability is an intangible asset Deferred Pension Cost. However, if the intangible asset account balance will exceed the amount of unrecognized prior service cost, the excess should be debited to a contra-equity account titled Excess of Additional Pension Liability Over Unrecognized Prior Service Cost. This account balance is reported on the balance sheet after Retained Earnings as a deduction in arriving at total stockholders' equity. The intangible asset Deferred Pension Cost is not amortized. The balance is adjusted each year on the basis of new calculations of the accumulated benefit obligation and the fair value of plan assets.

EXAMPLE

Assume the following information about a pension plan at a financial statement date:

Projected benefit obligation	$4,500,000
Accumulated benefit obligation	3,500,000
Fair value of plan assets	2,500,000
Unrecognized prior service cost	1,500,000
Accrued pension cost	500,000

There is no additional liability presently recognized in the accounts.

The minimum liability:

Accumulated benefit obligation	$3,500,000
Less: Fair value of plan assets	2,500,000
Minimum liability	$1,000,000

Additional liability required:

Minimum liability		$1,000,000
Less: Accrued pension cost at year-end		500,000
Additional liability		$ 500,000

The required adjusting entry:

Intangible Pension Asset	500,000	
Additional Pension Liability		500,000

If, instead of accrued pension cost of $500,000, the accounts reflected prepaid pension cost of $200,000, the additional liability would be:

Minimum liability		$1,000,000
Plus: Prepaid pension cost		200,000
Additional liability		$1,200,000

Adjusting entry:

Intangible Pension Asset	1,200,000	
Additional Pension Liability		1,200,000

In subsequent years, new calculations of the minimum liability would be made and an entry made to adjust the related accounts to reflect the required additional liability.

13.3 DETERMINATION OF PENSION COST

Six factors enter into the calculation of net pension cost (expense) for a period. The factors are:

1. Service cost.
2. Interest on the projected benefit obligation.
3. Prior service cost.
4. Actual return on plan assets.
5. Gains and losses.
6. Transition cost amortization.

SERVICE COST

Service cost is the actuarial present value of the pension benefits earned by employees in an accounting period as determined by the pension plan benefit formula. Service cost is calculated on assumed future compensation levels and thus each year increases the projected benefit obligation. The amount of service cost for a period will be determined by the plan actuary.

INTEREST ON THE PROJECTED BENEFIT OBLIGATION

This component is the interest on the projected benefit obligation (PBO) carried over from the prior year. The actuarial determination of the PBO is based on present value assumptions such that the present value of the beginning PBO increases during the year. This increase is the interest cost. The amount of interest cost for a period is calculated by multiplying the beginning of the year PBO by the interest (discount) rate used by the actuary in determining present value.

PRIOR SERVICE COST

Prior service cost is the cost of retroactive pension benefits resulting from plan initiation or amendment giving benefits to employees for services rendered before the plan initiation or amendment. The amount of such cost is the increase in the projected benefit obligation caused by the initiation or amendment of the plan.

Prior service cost should be amortized over the present and future periods affected. Two amortization methods are available: (1) the expected future years of service method, and (2) the straight-line method.

EXAMPLE

Assume prior service cost associated with a pension plan amendment amounts to $66,000. At the time of the amendment, the employer has 20 employees. It is expected that the workers will retire or terminate at the rate of two per year.

Amortization by expected future years of service method:

Amortization each year would be a fraction of the $66,000, with the fraction numerator being the number of remaining employees at the beginning of the year and the denominator being the sum of the number of employees at the beginning of each of the future years involved.

156

Year	Number of Employees	Amortization Fraction	Amortization Amount
1	20	20/110	$ 12,000
2	18	18/110	10,800
3	16	16/110	9,600
4	14	14/110	8,400
5	12	12/110	7,200
6	10	10/110	6,000
7	8	8/110	4,800
8	6	6/110	3,600
9	4	4/110	2,400
10	2	2/110	1,200
	110		$ 66,000

Amortization by straight-line method:

Amortization each year based on the average remaining service period of the employees.

Average remaining service period:

[110 (future service years) /20 (number of employees)] = 5.5 years

Annual amortization = $66,000/5.5 years = $12,000 per year

Years 1 – 5: Amortization = $12,000
Year 6   : Amortization = $ 6,000

ACTUAL RETURN ON PLAN ASSETS

The actual return on plan assets is the difference between the fair value of plan assets at the beginning and end of the period, adjusted for contributions and benefit payments. If this return is a gain, the amount is a reduction of pension expense. If a loss, it increases pension expense.

ILLUSTRATION

Fair value of plan assets at end of period		$12,000,000
Less: Fair value of plan assets at		
beginning of period		10,000,000
Increase in fair value of plan assets		$ 2,000,000
Deduct: Contributions to plan		
during period	$2,200,000	

Less: Benefits paid during period	800,000	1,400,000
Actual return on plan assets		$ 600,000

The $600,000 (a gain) would be a negative amount in calculating pension expense for the year.

GAINS AND LOSSES

These gains and losses, according to **SFAS 87**, are changes in the amount of either the projected benefit obligation or plan assets resulting from experience different from that assumed and from changes in assumptions. This component consists of: (1) the current period difference between the actual return on plan assets and the expected return, and (2) amortization of unrecognized net gain or loss from previous periods.

The expected return on plan assets is calculated by multiplying the market-related value of plan assets at the beginning of the year by the expected long-term rate of return on plan assets. The market-related value of plan assets is either the fair value or a calculated value that recognizes changes in fair value in a systematic and rational manner over not more than five years. If the actual return on plan assets (see calculation above) is greater than the expected return, this difference (deferred gain) is added in computing pension expense. If the actual return is less than expected, the difference (deferred loss) is deducted. The net effect of this procedure is to include in pension expense the **expected** return on plan assets. Recognition of the gain or loss is deferred as part of the end-of-the-period unrecognized net gain or loss for possible amortization in future periods.

EXAMPLE

Assume beginning-of-year plan assets of $10,000,000. The expected long-term rate of return on plan assets used by the plan actuary is 8%. Actual return on plan assets (see calculation in example above) is $600,000.

Expected return on plan assets:	
8% x $10,000,000	$800,000
Actual return on plan assets	600,000
Difference (loss)	200,000

The $200,000 loss would be deferred and deducted in calculating period pension expense. The effect is to use expected return in the calculation: ($600,000) actual return + ($200,000) loss = ($800,000) expected return.

The $200,000 would be part of the end-of-period unrecognized net gain or loss.

Amortization of unrecognized net gain or loss from previous periods is required if, at the beginning of the year, the amount of unrecognized net gain or loss exceeds 10 percent of the greater of the projected benefit obligation or the market-related value of plan assets. This 10% amount is sometimes referred to as the **corridor**. The minimum amount to be recognized through amortization is the excess outside the corridor divided by the average remaining service period.

EXAMPLE

Cumulative unrecognized net gain or loss, beginning of year	$40,000	loss
Projected benefit obligation, beginning of year	300,000	
Market-related value of plan assets, beginning of year	240,000	
Average remaining service period	10	years

Corridor:
Greater of: 10% x $300,000 = $30,000
             10% x $240,000 = $24,000
Therefore, use $30,000.

Amount subject to amortization:
$40,000 – $30,000 = $10,000
Minimum amortization:
$10,000 / 10 years = $1,000
(added to period pension cost)

TRANSITION COST AMORTIZATION

Transition cost arises at the time of a changeover in accounting for a pension plan from the previous standard (**APB Opinion 8**) to **SFAS 87**. The amount of the transition cost is the difference between the projected benefit obligation and the fair value of the pension plan assets, calculated at the beginning of the changeover year. The cost amount is reduced by any accrued pension liability previously recognized on the balance sheet (or increased by the amount of a prepaid asset). The transition cost must be amortized over the average remaining service period. If the average remaining service period is less than 15 years, the employer may elect to use 15 years.

EXAMPLE

Assumptions:

PBO at transition date	$3,000,000
Fair value of plan assets at transition date	2,000,000
Difference	$1,000,000
Less: Accrued pension liability previously recognized	100,000
Transition cost to be amortized	$ 900,000

Average remaining service period = 13 years

Employer elects to use 15-year amortization period.

Annual amortization = $900,000 / 15 = $60,000

The $60,000 would be added in computing period pension expense.

COMPREHENSIVE ILLUSTRATION

Assumptions:

At 1/1/x1:

Fair value of pension plan assets (= market-related value)	$2,000,000
Projected benefit obligation	2,574,000
Expected long-term rate of return on plan assets and actuary's discount rate	8%
Unrecognized cumulative net (gain)/loss	184,000
Prior service cost (to be amortized by straight-line over average remaining service period of 8 years)	160,000
Accrued pension liability	50,000
Accumulated benefit obligation	1,800,000
Transition cost being amortized at straight-line rate of $60,000 per year	

160

Information from actuaries and plan trustees for year ending 12/31/x1:

Service cost	$ 500,000
Funding by employer	600,000
Benefits paid during year	-0-
Fair value of plan assets 12/31/x1	2,740,000
Accumulated benefit obligation	2,200,000

Calculation of net periodic pension cost for 19x1:

(1) Service cost $500,000

(2) Interest on the beginning of year PBO:
    $2,574,000 x 8%   205,920

(3) Prior service cost amortization:
    $160,000 / 8   20,000

(4) Actual return on plan assets:

Fair value of plan assets 12/31	$2,740,000	
Less: Fair value of assets 1/1	2,000,000	
Increase in fair value of assets	$ 740,000	
Deduct:		
Contributions to plan		
during period	$600,000	
Less: Benefits paid	-0-	600,000
Actual return on plan assets		(140,000)

(5) Gains and losses:

Current period difference between		
actual and expected return:		
Expected return on plan assets:		
8% x $2,000,000	$160,000	
Actual return on plan assets	140,000	(20,000)

    Amortization of unrecognized net gain/loss
       Corridor:
              Greater of: 10% x $2,574,000 = $257,400
                           10% x $2,000,000 = 200,000
              Thus, corridor is $257,400
        Since $184,000 is less than $257,400, no amortization
        is required.

(6) Transition cost amortization   60,000

    Net periodic pension cost $ 625,920

Entries to record pension cost and funding:

Pension Expense	625,920	
Prepaid/Accrued Pension Cost		625,920
Prepaid/Accrued Pension Cost	600,000	
Cash		600,000

Accrued Pension Cost (liability) reported on balance sheet 12/31/ x1:

Balance 1/1/x1	$50,000
From entries above	
($625,920 – $600,000)	25,920
Balance 12/31/x1	$75,920

Test for minimum liability:

Accumulated benefit obligation 12/31	$2,200,000
Fair value of plan assets 12/31	2,740,000

Since accumulated benefit obligation does not exceed the fair value of plan assets at 12/31, no minimum liability exists.

Balance of unrecognized cumulative (gain)/loss at 12/31/x1:

Balance 1/1/x1		$184,000
Less:	Amortization	-0-
Add:	Current period difference between actual and expected return on plan assets (loss)	20,000
	Current period difference between actual and expected PBO (assumed)	-0-
Balance 12/31/x1		$204,000

CHAPTER 14

REVENUE RECOGNITION

14.1 GENERAL GUIDELINES

The FASB in its **Statements of Financial Accounting Concepts** has defined revenue and provided guidance for recognizing revenue. In **Concepts Statement No. 6**, revenue is defined as "inflows or other enhancements of assets of an entity or settlements of its liabilities (or a combination of both) from delivering or producing goods, rendering services, or other activities that constitute the entity's ongoing major or central operations."

A major accounting problem is identifying when revenue should be recognized. The production of revenue often involves a rather lengthy process, including activities such as acquiring raw materials, manufacturing a product, making sales, and collecting for the sales. The accounting question is to identify the critical event in this process which triggers recognition of the revenue. **Concepts Statement No. 5** gives general guidelines. Recognition is "the process of formally incorporating an item into the financial statements of an entity...." Revenue is to be recognized when it is (1) realized or realizable, and (2) earned. Revenue is **realized** when goods or services are exchanged for cash or claims to cash. Revenue is **realizable** when assets received in exchange are readily convertible to known amounts of cash or claims to cash. Revenue is **earned** when the entity has substantially accomplished what it must do to be entitled to the benefits represented by the revenues.

As a general rule, the critical event in the revenue process is at the

163

point of sale. At this point, the entity has substantially done all it must to be entitled to receive cash or claims to cash, or assets readily convertible to cash or claims to cash. Thus, revenue is generally recognized at the point of sale. However, there are some exceptions to this general rule, and they are discussed below.

14.2 LONG-TERM CONSTRUCTION-TYPE CONTRACTS

Major construction projects, such as construction of highways, bridges, and buildings, as well as certain other development-type projects, often require several years to complete. Technically, the point of sale in such projects is at the completion of the project. However, the contracts usually provide for partial payment to the contractor as work progresses, thus giving claims to cash before completion of the project. Two methods of accounting for such contracts are used: (1) the percentage-of-completion method, and (2) the completed contract method.

THE PERCENTAGE-OF-COMPLETION METHOD

In the percentage-of-completion method, income is recognized during the construction period on the basis of the percentage of the total work completed. This method requires estimates of the percentage of completion at the end of each accounting period. The estimates usually are calculated as the percentage of actual costs to date to estimated total costs. The estimates may also be based on engineering or architectural estimates.

ILLUSTRATION

Assume a contract to construct a building at a contract price of $2,000,000.

	19x1	19x2	19x3
Cost incurred to date	$ 600,000	$1,275,000	$1,650,000
Estimated cost to complete	1,000,000	425,000	-0-
Estimated total costs	$1,600,000	$1,700,000	$1,650,000

	19x1	19x2	19x3
Percentage of completion	600/1,600	1,275/1,700	1,650,1,650
	37.5%	75%	100%
Progress billings during year	$ 650,000	$ 700,000	$ 650,000
Collections on billings	450,000	500,000	1,050,000

Recognition of revenue & gross profit:
Contract Price x percent complete

	19x1	19x2	19x3
19x1: $2,000,000 x 37.5%	$750,000		
19x2: $2,000,000 x 75%		$1,500,000	
19x3: $2,000,000 x 100%			$2,000,000
Less: amount previously recognized:	-0-	750,000	1,500,000
Revenue to recognize	$ 750,000	$ 750,000	$ 500,000
Construction costs for year	600,000	675,000	375,000
Gross profit recognized	$ 150,000	$ 75,000	$ 125,000

Journal entries:

Costs incurred:

Construction in Progress	600,000	675,000	375,000
Cash (or payables, etc)	650,000	675,000	375,000

Progress billings:

Accounts Receivable	650,000	700,000	650,000
Billings on Contracts	650,000	700,000	650,000

Collections on billings:

Cash	450,000	500,000	1,050,000
Accounts Receivable	450,000	500,000	1,050,000

Recognition of income:

Construction in Progress	150,000	75,000	125,000
Contract Expenses	600,000	675,000	375,000
Contract Revenue	750,000	750,000	500,000

To close accounts in 19x3:

Billings on Contracts		2,000,000
Construction in Progress		2,000,000

Balance Sheet presentation:

	19x1	19x2	19x3
Costs and Recognized Profit in Excess of Billings (an asset):			
19x1: $600,000 + $150,000 − $650,000	$100,000		
19x2: $1,275,000 + $225,000 − $1,350,000		$150,000	
19x3: (Accounts closed)			-0-

As shown in the above illustration, on a particular contract, an excess of costs incurred to date plus profit recognized to date over the billings to date is reported as an asset. An excess of billings over costs and profit recognized to date on a contract would be reported as a liability. If a contractor has several projects in progress at a balance sheet date, with costs exceeding billings on some and billings exceeding costs on others, the contracts should be segregated. Those with excess of costs over billings would be reported on the asset side of the balance sheet, and the others on the liability side.

THE COMPLETED-CONTRACT METHOD

In the completed-contract method, no profit is recognized on a contract until it is completed. The accounting entries in this method parallel those for the percentage-of-completion method, except for the annual entry to recognize profit. At completion of the project, an entry is made to recognize the profit on the project.

ILLUSTRATION

Assume the data from the previous percentage-of-completion example.

At completion of the project, the following account balances would exist:

Construction in Progress	$1,650,000
Progress Billings	$2,000,000

Journal entry to recognize profit at completion:

166

Progress Billings	2,000,000	
Contract Expenses	1,650,000	
Construction in Progress		1,650,000
Contract Revenue		2,000,000

At any time during a long-term construction-type contract that there is a projected loss for the entire project, it must be recognized in full at that time.

EXAMPLE

Assume that, in the preceding illustration for the percentage-of-completion method, the 19x2 figures were as follows:

	19x2	
Costs incurred to date	$1,275,000	
Estimated cost to complete	850,000	
Estimated total costs	$2,125,000	
Projected loss on contract:		
Contract price	$2,000,000	
Estimated total costs	2,125,000	
Projected loss	$(125,000)	

Percentage of completion: 1,275/2,125 = 60%

Loss to recognize in 19x2:		
Projected loss		$(125,000)
Less: Profit recognized in 19x1		150,000
Loss to recognize in 19x2		$(275,000)
Revenue to recognize in 19x2:		
60% x $2,000,000		$1,200,000
Revenue previously recognized		750,000
Revenue to be recognized		$ 450,000
Expenses to recognize in 19x2:		
Total expenses equal to revenue		
recognized to date (= no profit)		$1,200,000
Loss expected on total contract		125,000
		$1,325,000
Less: Expenses previously recognized		600,000
Expenses to recognize		$ 725,000

Journal entry:

Contract Expenses	725,000	
Construction in Progress		275,000
Contract Revenue		450,000

If the completed-contract method had been used for this project, the following entry would be made at the end of 19x2. The amount is only for the $125,000 loss, since no profit would have been previously recognized.

Loss on Construction Contract	125,000	
Construction in Progress		125,000

At the end of 19x2, the balances in the inventory and billings accounts would be:

Construction in Progress	$1,150,000*
Billings on Contracts	1,350,000

The $200,000 excess of Billings on Contracts (over Construction in Progress) would be reported on the balance sheet as a liability.

Both the percentage-of-completion method and the completed-contract method are considered generally accepted methods. Current accounting standards, however, state the percentage-of-completion method is preferable when estimates of costs to complete and extent of progress toward completion of long-term contracts are reasonably dependable. Otherwise, the completed-contract method is preferable.

14.3 INSTALLMENT SALES

Sales are sometimes made with collection of the sale price to be in installments over an extended period of time. Under current GAAP, the revenue from such sales usually should be recognized in full at the point of sale. However, if collectability of the sales price is uncertain, or not reasonably assured, the **installment method** may be used to recognize revenue as collections are made.

---

* Percentage-of-completion: $600,000 + $150,000 + $675,000 − $275,000
Completed-contract: $600,000 + $675,000 − $125,000

ILLUSTRATION

A company made installment sales in 19x1 as follows:

Total installment sales, 19x1	$100,000
Cost of goods sold	60,000
Gross profit on sales	$ 40,000
Gross profit percentage:	
$40,000 / $100,000	40%

Collections on these sales:

19x1	$20,000
19x2	40,000
19x3 and later	40,000

19x1 entry to record sales:

Installment Accounts Receivable	100,000	
Deferred Gross Profit on		
Installment Sales		40,000
Inventory		60,000

Entry to record 19x1 collections:

Cash	20,000	
Installment Accounts Receivable		20,000

19x1 entry to record realized gross profit:

Deferred Gross Profit on Installment		
Sales (40% x $20,000)	8,000	
Realized Gross Profit on		
Installment Sales		8,000

The 19x1 balance sheet would show the balance of the deferred gross profit ($40,000 − $8,000 = $32,000) as contra to (deducted from) the installment accounts receivable balance.

19x2 entry to record collections of 19x1 installment sales:

Cash	40,000	
Installment Accounts Receivable		40,000

19x2 entry to record realized gross profit on 19x1 installment sales:

Deferred Gross Profit on Installment Sales (40% x $40,000)	16,000	
Realized Gross Profit on Installment Sales		16,000

Installment sales contracts may provide for **repossession** of the sold item if installment payments are not made.

ILLUSTRATION

Assume that an item sold in 19x1 (from above illustration) was repossessed in 19x2 when the buyer stops making payments.

Balance still owed at time of repossession	$400
Net realizable (market) value of the repossessed item	200

Entry:

Inventory of Used Merchandise	200	
Deferred Gross Profit on Installment Sales (40% x $400)	160	
Loss on Repossession	40	
Installment Accounts Receivable		400

If ultimate realization of revenue is highly uncertain or unpredictable, the **cost recovery method** may be used. In this method, all collections are applied first to recovery of cost, with revenue or profit recognized only after the total cost has been recovered.

14.4 OTHER REVENUE RECOGNITION ISSUES

RECOGNITION OF REVENUE WHEN RIGHT OF RETURN EXISTS

In some industries, sales are made in which the customer has the right to return the goods within a specified period. A **matching** problem is created when the sales are recorded in one accounting period and substantial amounts of returns occur in another. This problem can be met by estimating the returns and recording this estimate in the period that the sales are made. The FASB has stated in **SFAS 48** that this approach should be used if **all** of the following conditions are met. Otherwise, recognition of the revenue from the sales should be delayed until the conditions are met or the right of return expires. The conditions are:

1. The seller's price to the buyer is substantially fixed or determinable at the date of sale.

2. The buyer has paid the seller, or the buyer is obligated to pay the seller and the obligation is not contingent on resale of the product.

3. The buyer's obligation to the seller would not be changed in the event of theft or physical destruction or damage of the product.

4. The buyer acquiring the product for resale has economic substance apart from that provided by the seller.

5. The seller does not have significant obligations for future performance to directly bring about resale of the product by the buyer.

6. The amount of future returns can be reasonably estimated.

REVENUE FROM FRANCHISE FEES

In a **franchise agreement**, a **franchisor** grants certain rights to a **franchisee** regarding the operation of a business. For example, many fast-food restaurants are operated by franchisees. A franchise agreement usually involves an **initial franchise fee** payable by the franchisee to the franchisor, as well as **continuing franchise fees**. The major accounting issue involves the timing of recognition by the franchisor of the revenue from an initial franchise fee.

The FASB addressed the issue in **SFAS 45**. The initial franchise fee is, at least in part, payment to the franchisor for initial services, such as assistance in site selection, construction assistance, training of personnel, and promotion. **SFAS 45** states that the revenue from the initial franchise fee should be recognized when these initial services covered by the fee have been "substantially performed." Substantial performance means that the franchisor has no remaining obligation or intent to refund any of the cash received and has performed substantially all of the initial services.

CHAPTER 15

ACCOUNTING FOR INCOME TAXES

Corporations are subject to paying federal and state income taxes on their income. A deduction for income tax expense is therefore properly included on the income statement of a corporation. A major issue in accounting is the determination of the amount of expense to be shown and the proper reporting of the expense and the taxes payable.

15.1 INTERPERIOD INCOME TAX ALLOCATION

A company prepares a federal income tax return for a given period following the requirements of the **Internal Revenue Code**. The tax return includes a determination of **taxable income,** the amount which is used to determine the income tax payable for the period. The company's income statement also includes a determination of **income before taxes,** the amount from which income tax expense will be deducted. This amount is calculated on the basis of **generally accepted accounting principles (GAAP).** The amount of taxable income and the income before taxes (accounting income) are usually different, since each was determined on the basis of different measurement rules (Internal Revenue Code and GAAP). The objective in financial reporting is to report the tax expense and the related amounts of taxes paid or payable in the same period in which the related revenues, expenses, gains, and losses are reported on the income statement.

172

Accounting for income taxes is governed by **SFAS 96**, issued by the FASB. This pronouncement requires **comprehensive interperiod tax allocation** using the **asset and liability approach**. The FASB is presently considering the effective date for this requirement.

Differences between accounting income and taxable income may be classified as **permanent differences** and **temporary differences**. Permanent differences are defined as items which enter into determination either of taxable income but never accounting income, or accounting income but never taxable income. Temporary differences, according to **SFAS 96**, are differences between the tax basis of assets or liabilities and their reported amount in the financial statements, which will result in taxable or deductible amounts in future years when the reported amount of the assets or liabilities is recovered or settled, respectively. Temporary differences make necessary interperiod income tax allocation.

The following are examples of temporary differences:

TEMPORARY DIFFERENCES GIVING RISE TO FUTURE TAXABLE AMOUNTS:

   a.   Revenues and gains included in the tax return **after** recognition for accounting income. Example: Recognition in future years of gain on an installment sale on the installment basis after the total gain was recognized on the income statement at the time of the sale.

   b.   Expenses and losses included in the tax return **before** recognition for accounting income. Example: Use of accelerated depreciation on the tax return and straight-line on the income statement. The depreciation on the tax return will exceed that on the income statement in the early years of the asset's life, but will be less than the income statement in later years, giving rise to higher taxes.

TEMPORARY DIFFERENCES GIVING RISE TO FUTURE DEDUCTIBLE AMOUNTS:

   a.   Revenues and gains included in the tax return **before** recognition for accounting income. Example: Revenue collected in advance is recognized on the tax return when collected but on the

173

income statement later when earned. Since the tax was paid when the revenue was collected, the amounts recognized in the future on the income statement are deducted before determining taxes owed then.

b. Expenses and losses included in the tax return **after** recognition for accounting income. Example: Warranty costs are deducted on the income statement at the time the sale of the warranted products are made, but are deductible for tax purposes later when the warranties are honored. These later warranty expenditures would be deductible from accounting income to determine the amount subject to tax.

Taxable temporary differences existing at the end of a period create a deferred tax liability. Deductible temporary differences reduce future tax liability and may create a deferred tax asset, although recognition of such assets is limited by **SFAS 96**. Income tax expense for a period is the amount of income taxes currently payable plus or minus the change in the deferred tax liability plus or minus the change in the deferred tax asset.

Computation of the amount of deferred tax liability or asset at the end of a period and the income tax expense for the period requires a procedure whose basic points may be summarized as follows.

1. Identify the temporary differences which account for the difference between accounting income and taxable income.

2. Prepare a schedule of the temporary differences showing the taxable or deductible amounts which will result from each in the applicable future years. Determine the net taxable or deductible amount for each future year.

3. Carry back or carry forward net deductible amounts in particular years to offset taxable amounts in prior or subsequent years. Follow the requirements of the tax law for treatment of net operating losses. Current law permits carryback for three years and carryforward for fifteen years.

4. Calculate the amount of tax in each of the future years, assuming that the temporary differences are the only taxable amounts in those future years, and using currently enacted tax rates and laws.

5. Recognize a **deferred tax asset** for the tax benefit of net deductible amounts that could be realized by loss carryback from future years: (1) to reduce a current deferred tax liability and (2) to reduce taxes paid in the current or prior year.

6. Recognize a **deferred tax liability** for taxes payable in future years as calculated in Step 4.

7. Prepare a journal entry (or entries) to record income taxes for the period. The basic entry model is:

Income Tax Expense	(b) + (c) − (a)
Deferred Tax Asset	(a)
Deferred Tax Liability	(b)
Income Tax Payable	(c)

(a)   Amount from Step 5 above.
(b)   Amount from Step 6 above.
(c)   Amount from tax return for the year.

EXAMPLE #1

Deferred liability only, no carryback or carryforward.

A company's accounting income for the current year (19x1) is $10,000. Its taxable income is $8,000. The temporary differences accounting for this difference are $3,000 installment sale income taxable in future years as shown below and $1,000 warranty expense deductible in the future as shown below. Tax rates under currently enacted law are 19x1: 40%, 19x2: 40%, 19x3: 30%, 19x4: 30%. 19x1 is the first year the company is in operation.

Reconciliation of accounting income and taxable income and schedule of temporary differences:

	Current Year 19x1	19x2	19x3	19x4
Accounting income	$10,000			
Temporary differences:				
Installment sale	(3,000)	$1,000	$1,000	$1,000
Warranty expense	1,000	(1,000)		

	Current Year 19x1	19x2	19x3	19x4
Taxable income	$8,000	$ -0-	$1,000	$1,000
Tax rate	x 40%	x 40%	x 30%	x 30%
Income tax payable	$3,200			
Deferred tax liability	600	-0-	$ 300	$ 300

Journal entry:

Income Tax Expense	3,800	
Income Tax Payable		3,200
Deferred Tax Liability		600

EXAMPLE #2

Deferred liability only, carryback and carryforward.

A company's accounting income for the current year (19x1) is $10,000. Its taxable income is $9,000. The temporary differences accounting for this difference are $4,000 depreciation taken on the tax return greater than deducted on the income statement (taxable in future years), and $3,000 estimated expense recognized on the income statement, deductible in the future on the tax return. Tax rates under currently enacted law are 19x1: 40%, 19x2: 40%, 19x3: 30%, 19x4: 30%, 19x5: 30%, 19x6: 30%. 19x1 is the first year that the company is in operation.

Reconciliation of accounting income and taxable income and schedule of temporary differences:

	Current Year 19x1	19x2	19x3	19x4	19x5	19x6
Accounting income	$10,000					
Temporary differences:						
Depreciation	(4,000)	$ 200	$ 400	$1,000	$ 1,000	$1,400
Estimated Expense	3,000				(3,000)	
Taxable income	$ 9,000	$ 200	$ 400	$1,000	$(2,000)	$1,400
Carryback		(200)	(400)	(1,000)	1,600	
Carryforward					400	(400)

176

	Current Year 19x1	19x2	19x3	19x4	19x5	19x6
Balance	$ 9,000	$ -0-	$ -0-	$ -0-	$ -0-	$1,000
Tax rate	x 40%	x 40%	x 30%	x 30%	x 30%	x 30%
Income tax payable	$ 3,600					
Deferred tax liability	300	$ -0-	$ -0-	$ -0-	$ -0-	$ 300

Journal entry:

Income Tax Expense	3,900	
Income Tax Payable		3,600
Deferred Tax Liability		300

NOTE: If the carryforward to 19x6 had not used up the remaining loss of 19x5, no recognition would be given to the balance, since no taxable amounts from temporary differences are scheduled for 19x7 or later.

EXAMPLE #3

Deferred tax asset.

A company's accounting income for the current year (19x1) is $10,000. Its taxable income is $12,000. The temporary differences accounting for this difference are $1,000 installment sale income taxable in future years and $3,000 warranty expense deductible in the future. Tax rates under currently enacted law are 19x1: 40%, 19x2: 40%. 19x1 is the first year that the company is in operation.

Reconciliation of accounting income and taxable income and schedule of temporary differences:

	Current Year 19x1	19x2
Accounting income	$10,000	
Temporary differences:		
Installment sale	(1,000)	$1,000
Warranty expense	3,000	(3,000)
Taxable income	$12,000	$(2,000)
Tax rate	x 40%	

Income tax payable	$ 4,800	
Carryback	$ 2,000	2,000
	x 40%	
Deferred tax asset	$ 800	

Journal entry:

Income Tax Expense	4,000	
Deferred Tax Asset	800	
Income Tax Payable		4,800

NOTE: A deferred tax asset is recognized because the loss carryback from 19x2 would serve to reduce the taxes payable in 19x1 (the current year).

The above examples illustrate the basic accounting for income taxes required by **SFAS 96**. To simplify, each example assumes that calculations are being made for the first year of the company's operations. For subsequent years, the following relationship between income tax expense and deferred taxes would exist:

Income tax expense for current year =

Income tax payable on current year tax return
+/– **change** in deferred tax asset balance
+/– **change** in deferred tax liability balance

EXAMPLE

Income tax payable on current year tax return		$10,000
Deferred tax asset:		
At 1/1/x2	$ 4,000	
At 12/31/x2	3,000	
Deferred tax liability:		
At 1/1/x2	$ 6,000	
At 12/31/x2	7,000	

Journal entry:

Income Tax Expense	12,000	
Deferred Tax Asset		1,000
Deferred Tax Liability		1,000
Income Tax Payable		10,000

A net deferred tax asset or liability is reported on the balance sheet and classified into its current and noncurrent amounts. The current amount is the net deferred tax resulting from temporary differences which reverse in the next year after the balance sheet date. The remaining balance of the net deferred taxes is noncurrent. Deferred tax liabilities attributable to different taxing jurisdictions should not be offset.

15.2 INTRAPERIOD INCOME TAX ALLOCATION

Intraperiod tax allocation refers to the reporting of the income tax expense, determined as described above, on the financial statements for the current year. Specifically, it refers to allocation of the income tax expense to the major income statement items which give rise to the tax. The income statement items involved are income or loss from continuing operations, discontinued operations, extraordinary items, cumulative effect of accounting changes, and prior period adjustments.

The basic procedure for intraperiod tax allocation is to allocate to continuing operations the amount of tax expense or benefit calculated on the income or loss from continuing operations. Then the amount of tax expense allocated to the other income statement items is the incremental effect on income taxes that result from that item.

EXAMPLE

A company reports a loss from continuing operations of $2,000. Carryback of this loss would result in the refund of $400 of taxes paid in previous years. The income statement also reports an extraordinary gain of $3,000. The current year tax rate is 40%. Taxes payable for the year are $400 [40% x ($3,000 − $2,000)]. There are no temporary differences, so income tax expense equals income tax payable.

Allocation of income tax expense:

Total income tax expense	$400
Tax consequences of loss from continuing operations	(400)
Incremental tax consequences attributable to extraordinary gain	$800

Reporting of income tax expense on income statement:

Loss from continuing operations before income tax and extraordinary items		$(2,000)
Less: Income tax benefit from carryback of loss		400
Loss before extraordinary items		$(1,600)
Extraordinary items:		
Extraordinary gain (described)	$3,000	
Less: Applicable income tax expense	800	
Extraordinary gain net of income tax		2,200
Net Income		$ 600

When there is more than one category of items other than income from continuing operations, reference should be made to **SFAS 96** for special rules governing the determination of the incremental effect on income tax of each of the items.

CHAPTER 16

EARNINGS PER SHARE

Earnings per share (EPS) is regarded by many investors and other users of financial statements as a very important indicator of an entity's performance. The Accounting Principles Board in **APB Opinion 15** instituted the requirement that EPS be reported on the income statement and established rules for the calculation of this ratio. The FASB later suspended the requirement for **nonpublic** companies.

16.1 BASIC PRINCIPLES

Earnings per share is to be reported for common stock only. The basic formula for computing EPS is:

$$\frac{\text{Net income} - \text{dividends on preferred stock}}{\text{Weighted average number of common shares outstanding}}$$

Earnings per share should be reported in the following format:

Earnings per common share:
Income before extraordinary items	$ x.xx
Extraordinary gain (loss)	(.xx)
Net income	$ x.xx

The weighted average number of shares outstanding is computed each year for use in calculating EPS. The average takes into account changes in the number of shares outstanding during the year from events such as issuance of additional common shares, purchases of treasury stock, and stock dividends and splits. Changes occurring from stock dividends and splits are treated as retroactive adjustments to the number of shares, from the beginning of the period. Other changes are considered from the date of occurrence.

EXAMPLE

A corporation had 10,000 shares of stock outstanding on January 1, 19x1. The following changes occurred during the year:

Jan. 1	Shares outstanding	10,000	shares
July 1	2 for 1 stock split	20,000	
Sep. 1	Issued 6,000 additional shares	26,000	

Computation of weighted average shares:

Jan. 1 – July 1	10,000 shares		
	x 2 (to restate the split)		
	20,000	x 6 months	120,000
July 1 – Sep. 1	20,000 shares	x 2 months	40,000
Sep. 1 – Dec. 31	26,000 shares	x 4 months	104,000
Totals		12	264,000

Weighted average number of shares:

264,000 / 12 = 22,000

Note: If changes occur on other than the first day of the month, it may be necessary to compute the weighted average on the basis of the number of **days** rather than months.

If comparative statements are presented, EPS for previous years should be recomputed on the basis of the current year's capital structure.

The calculation and presentation of EPS may be complicated by the existence of **potentially dilutive** securities such as convertible debt or preferred stock and stock options. **APB Opinion 15** distinguishes between **simple capital structures** and **complex capital structures**. The calculation of EPS for each is discussed below.

16.2 CALCULATING EPS FOR SIMPLE CAPITAL STRUCTURES

A corporation has a **simple capital structure** if it has only common stock or common stock and other securities which are not potentially dilutive. Thus, a corporation whose capital includes common stock — and preferred stock which is not convertible into common stock — has a simple capital structure.

The calculation of EPS for a simple capital structure follows the general principles outlined above.

EXAMPLE

Assume a corporation has common stock outstanding as shown in the previous example (weighted average number of shares = 22,000). The company also has outstanding 2,000 shares of 6% preferred stock, $10 par, cumulative, nonconvertible, nonparticipating. No change in the number of preferred shares occurred during the year.

The company reported income as follows for the year:

Income before extraordinary items after taxes	$79,520
Extraordinary loss (net of tax)	(6,600)
Net income	$72,920

Earnings per share:

Income before extraordinary items ($79,520 − $1,200 pfd. dividend) / 22,000 shares	$ 3.56
Extraordinary loss ($6,600/22,000 shares)	(.30)
Net income	$ 3.26

16.3 CALCULATING EPS FOR COMPLEX CAPITAL STRUCTURES

A corporation has a **complex capital structure** for EPS purposes when it has securities such as convertible debt or stock options that have the potential for diluting earnings per share. A corporation with a complex capital structure is required to present the following two types of EPS information if either results in EPS that is 3 percent or more less than EPS calculated on the basis of the weighted average of common shares outstanding.

Primary earnings per share, based on outstanding common stock and dilutive **common stock equivalents.**

Fully diluted earnings per share, based on outstanding common stock, common stock equivalents, and other dilutive securities.

The general calculation formulas are:

Primary earnings per share =

(divided by)

$$\frac{\text{Net income less dividends on preferred stock (if the shares are not included in the denominator) + addback of interest on debt included in the denominator}}{\text{Weighted average shares of common stock outstanding + dilutive common stock equivalents}}$$

Fully diluted earnings per share =

(divided by)

$$\frac{\text{Net income less dividends on preferred stock (if the shares are not included in the denominator) + addback of interest on debt included in the denominator}}{\text{Weighted average shares of common stock outstanding + dilutive common stock equivalents + all other dilutive securities}}$$

Potentially dilutive securities are of two general types: Stock purchase contracts (options, warrants, rights, subscriptions) and convertible securities. Identification of common stock equivalents in each of these categories is described below. Securities identified as dilutive are assumed to have been exercised or converted at the beginning of the current period or at their issue date, if later.

STOCK PURCHASE CONTRACTS

Exercise of stock purchase contracts would result in the issuance of additional shares of stock. However, it would also generally result in cash being paid in to the corporation. Calculation of EPS assumes exercise of the purchase options. The **treasury stock method** is used as the assumption regarding the use by the corporation of the cash received. Purchase of treasury stock at the average market price for the period of the company's stock is assumed. If the option price is less than the market price, the result will be an assumed increase in the number of shares outstanding.

EXAMPLE

A corporation has outstanding options for the purchase of 5,000 shares of its common stock at $32 per share. The average market price of the stock during the year was $40 per share.

Assume exercise of options: Shares issued	5,000	shares
Cash received: 5,000 x $32 = $160,000		
Assumed purchase of treasury stock:		
$160,000 / $40 per share	4,000	shares
Common stock equivalents (assumed net increase in number of shares outstanding	1,000	shares

If the option price had been greater than the average market price, the number of shares purchased as treasury stock would have been greater than the number issued on exercise of option. Thus, the options would have an antidilutive effect (would increase EPS by reducing the denominator in the calculation). **APB Opinion 15** excludes antidilutive securities from calculation of EPS.

Special rules apply if the assumed number of shares purchased as treasury stock would exceed 20 percent of the number of shares of common stock outstanding at the end of the period.

CONVERTIBLE SECURITIES

Convertible debt and convertible preferred stock are considered common stock equivalents if, at the time of issuance and based on the market price of the securities at that time, the securities have an effective yield interest rate less than two-thirds of the Aa corporate bond interest rate at the date of issuance.

EXAMPLE

Assume the Aa bond interest rate is 11.4%.

2/3 x 11.4% = 7.6%

6% convertible preferred stock, $100 par value, 2,000 shares issued. Issue price $107 per share. Total issue price = $214,000. Each share is convertible into 2 shares of common stock.

Annual dividend = 2,000 shares x $6 per share = $12,000
Effective yield = $12,000 / $214,000 = 5.6%
Since 5.6% is less than 7.6%, these are common stock equivalents.

The number of shares of common stock issuable upon conversion would be 2,000 shares preferred x 2 shares common per share of preferred = 4,000 shares. This is the number of common stock equivalents and this number would be added to the denominator in the calculation of primary earnings per share. The preferred dividend would not be deducted for the numerator.

Note: In the case of convertible debt that qualifies as a common stock equivalent, the interest on the debt, net of income tax, would be added back to the net income in the numerator for the EPS calculation.

For fully diluted EPS, all dilutive securities are considered, including those that do not qualify as common stock equivalents. The number of shares to be added to the denominator would generally be calculated as above for primary earnings per share. Preferred dividends on additional dilutive convertible preferred stock would not be deducted in the numerator. Interest, after taxes, on additional dilutive convertible debt would be added back in the numerator. One exception in calculating fully diluted EPS is that in calculations for the treasury stock method the **end of the period market price per share** is used if it is higher than the average price for the period.

The objective in calculating EPS is to determine the maximum possible dilution. Thus, any securities which have the effect of increasing EPS are excluded from the computations. If a corporation has several potentially dilutive securities, several factors, including the order in which the dilutive effect of a particular security is tested, may affect the resulting EPS. Tests for antidilutive effect must be done separately for primary EPS and fully diluted EPS.

Comprehensive illustration:

Net income for year	$100,000
Weighted average shares of common stock outstanding	20,000

Additional aspects of capital structure:

6% preferred stock, nonconvertible, cumulative, nonparticipating, $100 par, 1,000 shares outstanding all year.

4% preferred stock, each share convertible into 4 shares of common stock, $100 par, 500 shares outstanding all year. Issued at 106 when Aa bond rate was 6%.

6% convertible bonds, $500,000 par outstanding, issued at par when the Aa bond interest rate was 7.8%. The bonds are convertible into 35 shares per 1,000 par value bond. The income tax rate is 40%.

Options outstanding providing for purchase of 1,000 shares of common stock at $20 per share. The average market price of the stock for the year was $25 and the price at the end of the period was $32.

Common stock equivalents:

The 6% preferred is **not** a CSE because it is not convertible.

The 4% preferred:
    2/3 test: 2/3 x 6% = 4%
    Yield on stock:
        Annual dividend = 4% x $50,000 = $2,000
        Issue price = 500 shares x $106 = $53,000
        Yield = $2,000 / $53,000 = 3.8%
    The yield (3.8%) is less than 4% (2/3 of Aa bond rate at issue).
    Therefore this preferred stock is a common stock equivalent.
    Number of shares to add to denominator:
        500 (pfd. shares) x 4 (conversion rate) = 2,000 shares

The convertible bonds:
    2/3 test: 2/3 x 7.8% = 5.2%
    Yield on bonds = 6% (issued at par)
    Therefore the bonds are **not** common stock
        equivalents, because the yield (6%) is greater
        than 5.2%, the 2/3 test.

Treasury stock method calculation on options:
Assumed exercise of options:
 1,000 shares of common issued
 $20,000 cash received (1,000 shares x $20)
Treasury stock assumed purchased:
 $20,000 / $25 per share = 800 shares
  (for primary EPS)
 $20,000 / $32 per share = 625 shares
  (for fully diluted EPS)
Number to add to denominator:
 1,000 − 800 = 200 (for primary EPS)
 1,000 − 625 = 375 (for fully diluted EPS)

Primary Earnings Per Share:

$$\frac{\$100{,}000\ (\text{net income}) - \$6{,}000\ (\text{dividend on preferred which is not a CSE})}{20{,}000\ \text{shares} + 2{,}000\ \text{shares} + 200\ \text{shares}} =$$

$$\frac{\$106{,}000}{22{,}200} = \$4.23$$

Fully Diluted Earnings Per Share:

$$\frac{\$100{,}000\ (\text{net income}) - \$6{,}000\ (\text{preferred dividend}) + \$18{,}000\ (\text{interest on bonds after taxes})}{20{,}000 + 2{,}000 + 375 + 17{,}500\ (\text{shares to be issued if bonds converted})} =$$

$$\frac{\$112{,}000}{39{,}875} = \$2.81$$

Test to determine if disclosure of primary and fully diluted EPS is required:

$$\frac{\$100{,}000\ (\text{net income}) - \$6{,}000\ (\text{preferred dividend}) - \$2{,}000\ (\text{preferred dividend})}{20{,}000\ (\text{weighted average number of shares})} =$$

188

$$\frac{\$92,000}{20,000} = \$4.60 \ (97\% = \$4.46)$$

Since both primary EPS ($4.23) and fully diluted EPS ($2.81) are more than 3% less than $4.60, disclosure is required.

CHAPTER 17

ACCOUNTING CHANGES

A company occasionally may encounter a situation which will require changes in its accounting. Examples of such situations are new standards issued by the FASB or changes in estimates of the useful lives of depreciable assets. A company may also discover errors in previous accounting which must be corrected. **APB Opinion 20** provides guidelines for making accounting changes and correcting errors.

17.1 TYPES OF ACCOUNTING CHANGES

APB Opinion 20 provides guidelines for handling each of the following situations.

Change in accounting principle: A change from one generally accepted accounting principle to another generally accepted accounting principle. Example: A change in depreciation method for previously recorded assets, such as from the declining balance method to the straight-line method.

Change in accounting estimate: A change in an estimate used in projecting the effects of future events on the financial statements. Example: A change in the estimate of the useful life or salvage value of a depreciable asset.

Change in reporting entity: A change in the composition of the reporting entity. Example: A change in the subsidiaries included in consolidated financial statements.

Correction of an error in previously issued financial statements: The correction of an error such as mathematical mistakes, mistakes in the application of accounting principles, or oversight or misuse of facts in previously issued statements. Example: Discovery in 19x2 of a mathematical error in the calculation of depreciation for an asset in 19x1.

17.2 ACCOUNTING FOR CHANGES IN ACCOUNTING PRINCIPLE

A change in accounting principle is a change from one generally accepted accounting principle to another. The term "accounting principle," according to **APB Opinion 20**, includes not only accounting principles and practices but also the methods of applying them. For most accounting changes, the cumulative effect of the change should be computed and reflected on the income statement in the year in which the change is made. For a few special cases identified in **APB Opinion 20**, retroactive restatement of all statements presented is required.

The cumulative effect of a change in accounting principle is the difference between the retained earnings at the beginning of the period in which the change is made and what the retained earnings would have been had the new accounting principle been used in the affected prior periods. That is, the difference between the use of the two principles in the affected periods up to the beginning of the current year less the related income tax effect. The cumulative effect should be reported on the income statement in the year in which the change is made as a separate item between the extraordinary item(s) and the net income.

EXAMPLE

A company which began operations in 19x1 used accelerated depreciation on its books and tax returns for 19x1 and 19x2. In 19x3, it changed to the straight-line method for financial reporting while continuing to use accelerated depreciation for tax purposes. The income tax rate for all three years is 40%. The company had 50,000 shares of common stock outstanding in each year.

	19x1	19x2	19x3
Income before cumulative effect of change in accounting principle	$50,000	$100,000	$125,000
Accelerated depreciation	15,000	20,000	20,000
Straight line depreciation	8,000	12,000	12,000

Cumulative effect of change in accounting principle:

Accelerated depreciation, 19x1-19x2	$35,000
Straight-line depreciation, 19x1-19x2	20,000
Difference (increase in reported income)	$15,000
Less: Income tax at 40%	6,000
Net cumulative effect	$ 9,000

Journal entry to record recognition of cumulative effect:

Accumulated Depreciation	15,000	
Cumulative Effect of Change in Accounting Principle		9,000
Deferred Income Taxes*		6,000

*Assumes differences in depreciation taxable in future at 40%.

Reporting of cumulative difference on comparable income statement for 19x3:

	19x3	19x2
Income before cumulative effect of change in accounting principle	$125,000	$100,000
Cumulative effect of change in accounting principle, net of $6,000 income taxes	9,000	—
Net income	$134,000	$100,000
Earnings per share:		
Income before cumulative effect of change in accounting principle	$2.50	$2.00
Cumulative effect of change in accounting principle	.18	—
Net income	$2.68	$2.00

Pro forma amounts assuming the
new depreciation method is
applied retroactively:

Net income	$125,000	$104,800 **
Earnings per share	2.50	2.10

**19x2 net income as reported	$100,000
Difference between straight-	
line and accelerated depreciation	
less 40% tax ($8,000 – $3,200)	4,800
	$104,800

APB Opinion 20 requires the presentation of pro forma amounts, as illustrated above, for all periods presented as if the new principle had been applied for all periods affected.

The special cases which require retroactive restatement are as follows:

1. A change from the LIFO method of inventory valuation to another method.

2. A change in the method of accounting for long-term construction-type contracts.

3. A change to or from the full-cost method of accounting in the extractive industries.

4. A change mandated by official pronouncement which requires retroactive restatement.

5. A change in accounting principle in connection with a forthcoming public offering of equity shares.

For these special cases, all statements presented should be restated using the new accounting principle. The cumulative effect of the change, net of taxes, should be recorded as an adjustment of the beginning balance of retained earnings of the earliest year presented.

There may be cases in which the cumulative effect of a change in accounting principle is not determinable. An example would be a change to the LIFO inventory method. If the cumulative effect is not determinable, the new accounting principle is used in the current year and no cumulative effect is reported.

The nature of and justification for a change in accounting principle must be disclosed in the financial statements of the period in which the change is made, with an explanation of why the new principle is preferable.

17.3 ACCOUNTING FOR CHANGES IN ACCOUNTING ESTIMATES

Estimates of the effects of future events are inherent in the accounting process. For example, estimates are made in accounting involving the collectability of accounts receivable and of the useful lives and salvage values of depreciable assets. As time passes, additional information may become available which indicates that previously used estimates need revision. **APB 20** states that the effects of a change in accounting estimate should be accounted for in the period of the change if that period only is affected, or in the period of the change and future periods if both are affected. No retroactive restatement of prior period financial statements or presentation of pro forma amounts is required.

EXAMPLE

A company acquired a building in 19x1 for a cost of $500,000. The original estimate of useful life was 30 years and salvage value $50,000. Depreciation on the building was recorded on a straight-line basis for ten years. At that time, a revised estimate of the building's useful life was a total of 40 years, with no change in estimated salvage value.

Depreciation for 19x1 – 19y0:

Original cost	$500,000
Less:Salvage value	50,000
Cost to be depreciated	$450,000
Annual depreciation ($450,000 / 30)	$ 15,000
Total depreciation (first 10 years)	$150,000

At beginning of 19y1:

Original cost	$500,000
Less: Accumulated depreciation	150,000
Book value	$350,000
Less: Salvage value	50,000

Remaining cost to be depreciated	$300,000
Remaining useful life:	
(40 years new estimated life	
less 10 years 19x1 – 19y0)	30 years
Revised annual depreciation	
($300,000 / 30 years)	$ 10,000

For 19y1 and remaining years of building's useful life, annual depreciation will be recorded at $10,000.

17.4 ACCOUNTING FOR CHANGES IN REPORTING ENTITY

A change may be made in the components included in the reporting entity for the current financial statements. Examples are a change to the presentation of consolidated financial statements when statements of the individual companies had been presented in prior years, or changing the specific subsidiaries included in the consolidated statements. APB 20 requires that for such a change the financial statements of all prior periods presented be restated to show the financial information for the new reporting entity for all periods.

17.5 CORRECTION OF ERRORS IN PREVIOUSLY ISSUED FINANCIAL STATEMENTS

APB 20 defines an error in financial statements as the result of "mathematical mistakes, mistakes in the application of accounting principles, or oversight or misuse of facts that existed at the time the financial statements were prepared." Errors must be distinguished from changes in accounting estimate, which result from new information or subsequent developments which permit revised estimates.

The correction of an error in previously issued financial statements is treated as a **prior period adjustment**. Such adjustments are reflected as adjustments of the opening balance of retained earnings of the period in which the adjustment is made. These adjustments are not reflected on the income statement of that period. If comparative statements are presented, adjustments of all affected amounts must be made to reflect retroactive application of the prior period adjustments.

CHAPTER 18

STATEMENT OF CASH FLOWS

The FASB, in **SFAS 95**, requires a Statement of Cash Flows be presented as one of the basic financial statements for fiscal years ending after July 15, 1988. The statement replaces the Statement of Changes in Financial Position which was previously required by generally accepted accounting principles.

18.1 OBJECTIVES OF THE STATEMENT OF CASH FLOWS

The purpose of the Statement of Cash Flows is to present information on the cash receipts and cash payments of an entity during a period so as to account for the change in cash and cash equivalents during the period. **Cash equivalents** are short-term, highly liquid investments that are both readily convertible to known amounts of cash and so near to maturity that they present insignificant risk of changes in value because of changes in interest rates. Investments with three months or less to maturity **at date of acquisition** qualify as cash equivalents.

Cash flows are classified in the statement as cash flows from operating activities, cash flows from investing activities, and cash flows from financing activities. **Operating activities** include all transactions and other events that are not defined as investing or financing activities. Operating activities involve transactions that enter into the determination of net income and generally involve producing and delivering goods and providing services. **Investing activities** include making and collecting loans and acquiring and disposing of debt or equity instruments and property, plant, and equipment and other productive assets. **Financing activities** include obtaining resources from owners and providing them with a return on, and a return of, their investments; borrowing money and repaying amounts borrowed, or otherwise settling the obligation; and obtaining and paying for resources obtained from creditors on long-term credit.

Examples of the activity categories are:

Operating activities:
    Cash received for sale of goods or services
    Cash received from dividends on Investments in equity securities
    Cash paid for inventory
    Cash paid to employees for services
    Cash paid for taxes

Investing activities:
    Cash received for sale of property, plant, and equipment
    Cash paid for purchase of property, plant, and equipment
    Cash received for sale of investment in debt or equity securities
    Cash paid to acquire investment in debt or equity securities

Financing activities:
    Cash received for sale of corporation's own stock
    Cash received through issuance of debt
    Cash paid to stockholders as dividends
    Cash paid to retire debt

In general, operating activities involve income statement items. Investing activities involve changes in long-term **assets**. Financing activities involve **long-term liabilities** and **stockholders' equity**.

The following illustrates the basic model of the statement.

X CORPORATION
Statement of Cash Flows
For the Year Ending December 31, 19xx

Increase (Decrease) in Cash and Cash Equivalents

Cash flows from operating activities:
    Cash received from customers $ xx

Cash paid to suppliers and employees	(xx)	
Income taxes paid	(xx)	
Net cash provided by operating activities		$ xx
Cash flows from investing activities:		
Proceeds from sale of facility	$ xx	
Capital expenditures	(xx)	
Net cash used in investing activities		(xx)
Cash flows from investing activities:		
Proceeds from issuance of long-term debt	$ xx	
Proceeds from issuance of common stock	xx	
Net cash provided by financing activities		xx
Net increase in cash and cash equivalents		xx
Cash and cash equivalents at beginning of year		xx
Cash and cash equivalents at end of year		$ xx

Reconciliation of net income to net cash provided by operating activities:

Net income	$ xx	
Adjustments to reconcile net income to net cash provided by operating activities:		
Depreciation and amortization	$ xx	
Provision for losses on accounts receivable	xx	
Increase in accounts receivable	(xx)	
Decrease in inventory	xx	
Increase in prepaid expenses	(xx)	
Decrease in accounts payable and accrued expenses	(xx)	
Total adjustments		xx
Net cash provided by operating activities		$ xx

Supplemental schedule of noncash investing and financing activities:

Additional common stock was issued upon conversion of $xx of long-term debt.

Disclosure of accounting policy:

For purposes of the statement of cash flows, all highly-liquid debt instruments purchased with a maturity of three months or less are considered cash equivalents.

18.2 PRESENTATION OF CASH FLOWS FROM OPERATING ACTIVITIES

SFAS 95 recognizes two methods for reporting cash flows from operating activities. The **direct method** reports the cash flows resulting from each income statement item or category. It is a cash basis statement of cash receipts and payments resulting from operations. The method requires conversion of the accrual basis income statement into a cash basis statement. The **indirect method**, on the other hand, does not report cash flows from individual operating categories, but rather determines net cash flow from operating activities through a reconciliation or adjustment process. The process starts with the accrual basis net income from the income statement which is then converted to a cash basis by adding or subtracting changes in certain related balance sheet accounts. The difference between the two methods is a matter of presentation, since both methods arrive at the same net cash flow.

The FASB in **SFAS 95** expressed a preference for the direct method of presentation. The indirect method may be used, however. If the direct method is used, a separate reconciliation of net income to net cash flow from operating activities must be provided as part of the statement of cash flows. This reconciliation is the same as the indirect method of presentation.

18.3 PREPARATION OF THE STATEMENT OF CASH FLOWS

The following basic steps may be used to prepare the statement of cash flows:

1.   Determine the net change in the cash balance from the end of last year to the end of the current year by referring to the comparative balance sheet. This is the amount for which the statement of cash flows must account.

2.   Calculate the net cash flow from operating activities, using either the direct or indirect methods. This calculation requires use of the income statement and an analysis of changes in related balance sheet accounts.

3. Analyze changes in other balance sheet accounts to identify cash flows from investing and financing activities.

4. Arrange the information obtained from steps 1, 2, and 3 into a formal statement of cash flows.

The following is an illustration of the application of this procedure.

Income Statement, for year ended 12/31/x2:

Net sales	$60,000
Cost of goods sold	30,000
Gross profit on sales	$30,000
Salaries expense	5,000
Depreciation expense	4,000
General and administrative expenses	7,000
Income before taxes	$14,000
Income taxes	6,000
Net income	$ 8,000

Comparative Balance Sheet:

	12/31/x2	12/31/x1	Net change
Cash	$ 8,000	$ 3,000	$ 5,000
Accounts receivable	16,000	12,000	4,000
Inventory	6,000	8,000	(2,000)
Prepaid expenses	1,000	2,000	(1,000)
Plant and equipment	30,000	20,000	10,000
Accumulated depreciation	(12,000)	(8,000)	(4,000)
Total assets	$49,000	$37,000	$12,000
Accounts payable	$ 8,000	$ 6,000	$ 2,000
Income taxes payable	6,000	4,000	2,000
Accrued salaries	1,000	2,000	(1,000)
Common stock $10 par	20,000	15,000	5,000
Retained earnings	14,000	10,000	4,000
Total liabilities and stockholders' equity	$49,000	$37,000	$12,000

To calculate the net cash flow from operating activities:

Direct method:

1. Convert sales to cash collected from customers:

Accounts receivable, 12/31/x1	$12,000
Add: Sales	60,000
	$72,000
Less: Accounts receivable, 12/31/x2	16,000
Cash collected	$56,000

2. Convert cost of goods sold to cash paid to suppliers:

Purchases:

Inventory, 12/31/x2	$ 6,000
Add: Cost of goods sold	30,000
	$36,000
Less: Inventory, 12/31/x1	8,000
Purchases	$28,000

Payments for purchases:

Accounts payable, 12/31/x1	$ 6,000
Add: Purchases	28,000
	$34,000
Less: Accounts payable, 12/31/x2	8,000
Cash paid to suppliers	$26,000

3. Convert salaries expense to cash paid for salaries:

Accrued salaries, 12/31/x1	$ 2,000
Add: Salaries expense	5,000
	$ 7,000
Less: Accrued salaries, 12/31/x2	1,000
Cash paid for salaries	$ 6,000

4. The depreciation expense is a non-cash expense.

5. Convert general and administrative expense to cash paid:

Prepaid expense, 12/31/x2	$ 1,000
Add: General and administrative expense	7,000
	$ 8,000
Less: Prepaid expense, 12/31/x1	2,000
Cash paid for general and admin. expense	$ 6,000

6. Convert income tax expense to cash paid for income taxes:

Income tax payable, 12/31/x1	$ 4,000
Add: Income tax expense	6,000
	$10,000

Less: Income tax payable, 12/31/x2	6,000
Cash paid for income taxes	$ 4,000

Therefore, the net cash flow from operating activities:

Cash received from customers	$56,000
Cash paid to suppliers	(26,000)
Cash paid to employees	(6,000)
Cash paid for general & admin. expense	(6,000)
Cash paid for income taxes	(4,000)
Net cash provided by operating activities	$14,000

Analyze changes in other balance sheet accounts:

Plant and equipment increased $10,000. The company purchased new equipment for cash during the year at a cost of $10,000. Purchase of plant and equipment is an investing activity.

Cash flow from investing activities:	
Cash paid for new equipment	$(10,000)

The company issued at par for cash 500 shares of common stock. Issuance of stock is a financing activity.

Cash flow from financing activities:	
Issuance of common stock	$ 5,000

The company paid cash dividends during the year of $4,000. Payment of dividends is a financing activity.

Cash flow from financing activities:	
Payment of dividends	$ (4,000)

The formal statement is prepared from above information.

EXAMPLE CORPORATION
Statement of Cash Flows
for the year ending December 31, 19x2

Increase (Decrease) in Cash and Cash Equivalents

Cash flows from operating activities:

Cash received from customers	$56,000
Cash paid to suppliers	(26,000)
Cash paid to employees	(6,000)
Cash paid for gen. & admin. expense	(6,000)
Cash paid for income taxes	(4,000)

Net cash provided by operating activities		$14,000
Cash flows from investing activities:		
Cash paid for new equipment		(10,000)
Cash flows from financing activities:		
Issuance of common stock	$ 5,000	
Payment of dividends	(4,000)	
Net cash provided by financing activities		1,000
Net increase in cash and cash equivalents		$ 5,000
Cash and cash equivalents, 12/31/x1		3,000
Cash and cash equivalents, 12/31/x2		$ 8,000

The indirect method of determining net cash flows from operating activities:

1. The increase in accounts receivable ($4,000) is deducted from net income to convert to cash collected from customers. Sales for the year were $4,000 greater than collections, resulting in the $4,000 increase in accounts receivable.

2. The decrease in inventory ($2,000) is added back to net income. The decrease indicates $2,000 more in goods were used than were purchased during the current year.

3. The decrease in prepaid expense ($1,000) is added back to net income. The decrease indicates $1,000 more general and administrative expense was recognized during the year than was paid.

4. The increase in accumulated depreciation ($4,000) is added back to net income. The depreciation expense results in no cash payment.

5. The increase in accounts payable ($2,000) is added back to net income. The increase indicates $2,000 more in goods were purchased than were paid for during the year.

6. The increase in income tax payable ($2,000) is added back to net income. The increase indicates $2,000 more income tax expense was recognized during the year than was paid.

7. The decrease in accrued salaries ($1,000) is deducted from

net income. The decrease indicates $1,000 more in salaries were paid than were recognized as expense during the year.

The resulting section of the statement would be:

Cash flows from operating activities:	
Net income	$ 8,000
Adjustments to reconcile net income to net cash provided by operating activities:	
Increase in accounts receivable	(4,000)
Decrease in inventory	2,000
Decrease in prepaid expense	1,000
Depreciation expense	4,000
Increase in accounts payable	2,000
Increase in taxes payable	2,000
Decrease in accrued salaries	(1,000)
Net cash provided by operating activities	$14,000

Some transactions of a financing or investing nature may occur during a period and not result in cash receipts or payments. An example would be the acquisition of land by a corporation by issuing shares of the corporation's stock. **SFAS 95** requires that such noncash transactions be disclosed on the statement of cash flows in either a schedule or narrative format.

EXAMPLE

Supplemental schedule of noncash investing and financing activities:

Land with a fair value of $100,000 was acquired by issuing additional common stock.

CHAPTER 19

EFFECTS OF CHANGING PRICES

The measuring unit in financial reporting is the monetary unit, the dollar in the United States. Changing price levels, generally increasing prices (inflation), are a fact of life in the United States and around the world. Changes in price levels mean changes in the purchasing power of monetary units, which therefore means that these monetary units are not a stable measurement unit for financial reporting. Questions thus are raised about the comparability of measurements made at different times with a measuring unit which is not stable.

19.1 APPROACHES TO THE PROBLEM OF CHANGING PRICES

The traditional accounting model which generally does not recognize changes in the value of the monetary unit is the historical cost model, or more specifically, the **historical cost/nominal dollars** model. Transactions are recorded in terms of cost and no adjustments are made for changes in prices that occur after the transaction is recorded.

Approaches which have been suggested that do consider changes in prices are:

1. **Historical cost/constant dollars:** Maintains financial statement items in terms of dollars of the same purchasing power. Historical cost amounts are adjusted for changes in the purchasing power of the dollar through use of a price index, specifically, the Consumer Price Index.

2. **Current cost/nominal dollars:** Reports financial statement items in terms of specific current cost of individual items, stated in current dollars without specific consideration of changes in the general purchasing power of the dollar.

3. **Current cost/constant dollars:** Reports financial statement items in terms of specific current cost of individual items, but in dollars of the same purchasing power. Changes in specific prices and the general price level are both considered and reported separately.

Concepts of **capital maintenance** are related to the approaches described above. The general principle is that no income exists unless capital (net assets) are maintained. Income is the amount in excess of what is required to be as well off at the end of a period as at the beginning.

The **financial capital maintenance** concept measures capital in terms of dollars, either nominal dollars or constant dollars. Income is recognized only after the dollar investment in net assets or capital is maintained. This concept is the basis for the traditional view of financial reporting.

The **physical capital maintenance** concept measures capital in terms of physical productive capacity. Income is recognized only after the current replacement cost of physical capacity is covered. Current cost accounting is based on the physical capital maintenance concept.

19.2 HISTORICAL COST/CONSTANT DOLLARS ACCOUNTING

Financial statement items can be converted from historical cost in nominal dollars to constant dollars by using the Consumer Price Index. The calculation is as follows:

Historical cost in restated dollars of constant purchasing power =

$$\text{Historical cost (nominal dollars)} \quad X \quad \frac{\text{Price index of period adjusting to}}{\text{Price index of period adjusting from}}$$

EXAMPLE

Price indexes:

12/31/x1	105
12/31/x2	110
12/31/x3	118

Asset acquired on 12/31/x1 for $10,000.

Asset restated for financial statement at 12/31/x3:

$10,000 x 118/105 = $11,238

The principle is that the $11,238 at 12/31/x3 represents the same purchasing power as the $10,000 cost at 12/31/x1.

The effects of changing price levels are different for monetary items than for nonmonetary items. **Monetary items** are cash, assets representing a claim to a fixed amount of cash in the future (such as accounts receivable), and liabilities representing an obligation to pay a fixed amount of cash in the future (such as accounts payable). **Nonmonetary items** are assets whose price may change over time (such as inventories) and liabilities involving obligations to provide fixed amounts of goods or services (such as revenue received in advance). Holding of monetary items during periods of price level change results in **purchasing power gains and losses.**

EXAMPLE

Price indexes:

12/31/x1	100
12/31/x2	110

$100 cash is acquired on 12/31/x1 and held until 12/31/x2.

Cash needed on 12/31/x2 to have same purchasing power as on 12/31/x1:

$100 x 110/100 = $110

Since the cash is fixed in nominal value at $100, a $10 purchasing power **loss** has occurred: $110 − $100 = $10.

Since nonmonetary items do not represent fixed dollar amounts, no purchasing power gain or loss occurs on these items. In the example above, if the asset acquired on 12/31/x1 were a camera, for example, its original cost could be restated to $110 at 12/31/x2 to represent the item in dollars of equivalent purchasing power. This restatement would be made since the camera's value is not fixed in dollars but retains its purchasing power value as the price level changes.

The steps in the process of preparing financial statements on a historical cost/constant dollar basis are:

1. Classify items on the financial statements as monetary and nonmonetary.

2. Restate the balance sheet to constant dollars. Monetary items are not restated. Nonmonetary items are restated using the ratio of the price index at the statement date over the price index at the date of the transaction in which each item was acquired.

3. Restate the income and retained earnings statements to constant dollars. All items are nonmonetary and are restated using the ratio of the price index at the end of the period over the price index at the transaction date. Items which are incurred generally evenly over the period (such as sales and cost of goods sold) may be restated using the average price index for the period as the denominator of the ratio.

4. Compute the purchasing power gain or loss on net monetary items and include on the restated income statement.

19.3 CURRENT COST ACCOUNTING

In current cost accounting, each financial statement item is stated in terms of its specific current cost. **Current cost** usually means the amount that would have to be paid currently to replace the item in its existing condition. Several methods are available for determining current cost, including reference to current invoice prices, vendor price lists or quotations. Also, specific price indexes, either externally or internally generated, for the item or class of items, may be used to estimate current cost.

The current cost/nominal dollars approach uses current cost without consideration for changes in the general price level. The FASB, in SFAS 89, recommends disclosure of information on basically a current cost/constant dollars basis. This approach recognizes changes in the general price level as well as changes in specific prices (current cost).

Current cost accounting recognizes **holding gains and losses** resulting from changes over time of the current cost of assets.

EXAMPLE

An asset is acquired on 12/31/x1 for $10,000. On 12/31/x2 the current cost of the asset is $12,000. The unrealized holding gain for 19x2 is $2,000.

A holding gain or loss is **realized** when assets are used or consumed during a period. **Unrealized** holding gains and losses relate to assets held during a period and still held at the end of the period. In current cost/constant dollars accounting, holding gains are measured **net of general price level changes**.

EXAMPLE

Price indexes:
    12/31/x1   110
    12/31/x2   120

Asset acquired on 12/31/x1 for $10,000. Current cost at 12/31/x2 is $12,000.

Asset cost at 12/31/x1 restated to 12/31/x2 dollars:

$10,000 x 120/110 = $10,909

Holding gain:

$12,000 (12/31/x2 current cost) − $10,909 = $1,091

The basic procedure for preparing financial statements on a current cost/constant dollars basis is as follows:

1. Restate the balance sheet to current cost. Monetary items are presented the same as for historical cost/constant dollar accounting. Nonmonetary items are restated to current cost, using

209

appropriate methods of determining current cost. Stockholders' equity is a balancing amount.

2. Restate the income statement to a current cost basis. Calculate purchasing power gain or loss on monetary items, the effect on nonmonetary assets of changes in the general price level, and the effects of changes in current cost on specific assets (holding gains and losses). These items are included on the current cost/ constant dollars income statement.

Note: The details of preparation of complete financial statements on an historical cost/constant dollars or current cost/constant dollars basis are rather complex, and the reader desiring to learn these details should refer to an intermediate accounting textbook.

19.4 THE FASB POSITION ON CHANGING PRICE LEVELS

Both the Accounting Principles Board and the Financial Accounting Standards Board, over the last thirty years, have made several attempts to arrive at a standard and required method of recognizing the effects of changing prices on the financial statements. Most notable of these efforts was **SFAS 33**, in which the FASB conducted an experiment requiring certain large companies to present supplementary information concerning the effects of price changes. After several years of this experiment, it was decided that the **SFAS 33** information was not sufficiently useful to be required for all financial reporting. In 1986, **SFAS 89** was issued, which encourages but does not require the presentation of certain supplementary information on the effects of changing prices.

SFAS 89 states that those entities which elect to present supplementary information on the effects of changing prices should report the following for each of the five most recent years:

1. Net sales and other operating revenues.

2. Income from continuing operations on a current cost basis.

3. Purchasing power gain or loss on net monetary items.

4. Increase or decrease in the current cost or lower recover-

able amount of inventory and property, plant, and equipment, net of inflation.

5. The aggregate foreign currency translation adjustment on a current cost basis, if applicable.

6. Net assets at year-end on a current cost basis.

7. Income per common share from continuing operations on a current cost basis.

8. Cash dividends declared per common share.

9. Market price per common share at year-end.

In addition, if for the current year, income from continuing operations on a current cost/constant dollars basis differs significantly from income as reported on the financial statements, other disclosures are required by SFAS 89.

CHAPTER 20

FINANCIAL REPORTING PROBLEMS

20.1 INTERIM REPORTING

Many entities prepare financial statements covering periods of time less than one year. Such statements are called **interim financial statements. APB Opinion 28** presents guidelines for the preparation of such statements.

The general principle governing interim reports is that each interim period should be viewed primarily as an integral part of an annual period rather than as a separate accounting period. In general, the accounting principles and practices used in interim statements should be the same as those used for annual statements. Specific application of these general principles is discussed below.

Revenue from products sold or services rendered should be recognized during an interim period on the same basis as followed for the full year. Costs directly associated with the revenue recognized (example: cost of goods sold) should be recognized in the same interim period in which the revenue was recognized. All other costs and expenses are recognized for interim statements on the same basis as for annual statements, except that when a cost clearly benefits more than one interim period, the cost should be allocated to the interim periods benefited. An example of a cost benefiting more than one interim period would be an annual plant shutdown for repairs. If such repairs occur in the first quarter of the annual period, the expense should be allocated to all quarters rather than being charged totally against the first quarter.

In measuring cost of goods sold for an interim period, **APB Opinion 28** permits certain exceptions to the general rule of following the principles used in annual statements. These exceptions are:

1. The gross profit method may be used to estimate inventories.

2. If a LIFO liquidation of a base period inventory occurs at an interim date but the inventory is expected to be replaced before the end of the annual period, the inventory at the interim date should not reflect the LIFO liquidation.

3. If the market value of inventory at an interim date is lower than cost but the market value is expected to rise above cost by the end of the annual period, the temporary decline need not be recognized as a loss for the interim period.

4. Standard cost variances which are expected to be absorbed by the end of the annual period should be deferred at interim reporting dates.

Requirements for interim reporting of other items may be summarized as follows:

Extraordinary items: Report in interim period in which incurred.

Discontinued operations: Report in interim period in which incurred.

Changes in accounting principle requiring recognition of cumulative effect:

Change made in first interim period – cumulative effect recognized in that period.

Change made after first interim period – no cumulative effect recognized in period of change. The cumulative effect as of the beginning of the year should be determined and accumulated income for interim periods of that year prior to the period of the change should be restated.

Income taxes: Income tax expense for an interim period is determined on the basis of an estimated effective tax rate for the full year. The expense for a particular interim period is: year-to-date income multiplied by estimated effective tax rate minus expense recognized in previous interim periods that year.

EXAMPLE

Quarter	(1) Interim Income Before Income Taxes	(2) Year to date Income	(3) Estimated Effective Tax Rate for Year	(4) [(2) x (3)] Year-to- date Income Tax Expense	(5) Expense Recognized In Previous Quarters	(6) [(4) – (5)] Current Quarter Expense
1	$ 60,000	$ 60,000	32%	$19,200	$ –0–	$19,200
2	80,000	140,000	32%	44,800	19,200	25,600
3	40,000	180,000	28%	50,400	44,800	5,600
4	100,000	280,000	34%	95,200	50,400	44,800

20.2 SEGMENT REPORTING

Some reporting entities consist of segments operating in different industries, in foreign countries, and with major customers. **SFAS 14** requires that additional segment information be provided under specified circumstances and stipulates the format of the required disclosures.

INDUSTRY SEGMENTS

SFAS 14 requires certain disclosures for industry segments which qualify as **reportable segments.** An industry segment is reportable if at least one of the following tests is met:

1. Segment revenue is 10 percent or more of the combined revenue of all the entity's segments. Revenue includes both sales to unaffiliated customers and intersegment sales or transfers.

2. Segment operating profit or loss is 10 percent or more of the greater of the combined operating profit of all segments reporting a profit or the combined operating loss of all segments reporting a loss. Operating profit or loss is revenue minus all operating expenses.

3. A segment's identifiable assets are 10 percent or more of the combined identifiable assets of all segments. Identifiable assets

are those assets used by the segment, including both assets used exclusively by the segment and an allocated portion of assets used jointly by two or more segments.

EXAMPLE

Absolute amount of operating profit of those segments reporting a profit = $20,000 + $60,000 + $20,000 = $100,000

Absolute amount of operating loss of those segments reporting a loss = $5,000 + $15,000 = $20,000

Segment	Revenue	Operating Profit (Loss)	Identifiable Assets
A	$100,000	$20,000	$ 200,000
B	40,000	(5,000)	90,000
C	150,000	60,000	300,000
D	25,000	(15,000)	60,000
E	180,000	20,000	400,000
Total	$495,000	$80,000	$1,050,000

Segment A:
Test 1: 10% of total revenue = 10% x $495,000 = $49,500
    Segment revenue ($100,000) is greater.
Test 2: 10% of combined operating profit = $10,000
    (Combined profit is greater than combined loss)
    Segment profit ($20,000) is greater.
Test 3: 10% of identifiable assets = $105,000
    Segment assets ($200,000) are greater.

Segment A meets all tests and is a reportable segment.

Segment B:
Test 1: Revenue is **not** greater than 10%.
Test 2: Loss is **not** greater than 10%.
Test 3: Assets are **not** greater than 10%.

Segment B is **not** a reportable segment.

Segment C:
Test 1: Revenue is greater than 10%.
Test 2: Profit is greater than 10%.
Test 3: Assets are greater than 10%.

Segment C is a reportable segment.

Segment D:
Test 1: Revenue is **not** greater than 10%.
Test 2: Loss is greater than 10%.
Test 3: Assets are **not** greater than 10%.

Segment D is a reportable segment, since one test is met.

Segment E:
Test 1: Revenue is greater than 10%.
Test 2: Profit is greater than 10%.
Test 3: Assets are greater than 10%.

Segment E is a reportable segment.

Additionally, **SFAS 14** requires that reportable segments must represent a substantial portion of the enterprise's total operations. The test is that combined revenue from sales to unaffiliated customers of all reportable segments must constitute at least 75 percent of the combined revenue from sales to unaffiliated customers of all industry segments. If this test is not met, additional reportable segments are to be identified until the 75 percent test is met. However, the number of segments should not be so great as to make the segment information overly detailed. **SFAS 14** suggests that ten reportable segments is a practical limit. If this limit is passed, closely related industry segments should be combined into broader reportable segments to the extent necessary to reduce the number of reportable segments while still meeting the 75 percent test.

The following information is to be presented for each reportable segment and in the aggregate for other segments:

1. Revenue, with sales to unaffiliated customers and sales or transfers to other segments of the entity separately disclosed.

2. Operating profit or loss.

3. Identifiable assets.

4. Depreciation, depletion, and amortization expense.

5. Capital expenditures for property, plant, and equipment.

6. Equity in the net income from, and investment in the net assets of, unconsolidated subsidiaries and other equity method investees whose operations are vertically integrated with those of the segment.

7. Effects of the changes in accounting principle.

FOREIGN OPERATIONS

Information about an entity's foreign operations must be presented if either of the following conditions is met:

1. Revenue from foreign operations sales to unaffiliated customers is 10 percent or more of consolidated revenue.

2. Identifiable assets of the foreign operations are 10 percent or more of total assets.

If foreign operations are conducted in two or more geographic areas, information must be presented separately for each geographic area which meets the above conditions, with information about the remaining areas, if any, presented in the aggregate.

The following information is required to be presented:

1. Revenue, with sales to unaffiliated customers and sales or transfers between geographic areas presented separately.

2. Operating profit or loss.

3. Identifiable assets.

If the amount of sales by an entity's domestic operations to foreign customers is 10 percent or more of total revenue from sales to unaffiliated customers, the amount must be separately presented.

MAJOR CUSTOMERS

If 10 percent or more of an entity's revenue comes from sales to any single customer, the amount of revenue from each such customer must be disclosed. The customer name need not be disclosed. The industry segment making the sales must be disclosed. This information must be presented even if there are no reportable industry segments or foreign operations.

CHAPTER 21

FINANCIAL STATEMENT ANALYSIS

21.1 OBJECTIVES OF FINANCIAL STATEMENT ANALYSIS

The objective of financial reporting is the presentation of information useful in the making of decisions. The objective of financial statement analysis is the identification of information in financial statements that is relevant to a particular decision and the determination of significant trends and relationships that relate to that decision.

21.2 ANALYTICAL TECHNIQUES

PERCENTAGE ANALYSIS

One analytical technique involves converting the absolute dollar amounts on the financial statements into percentage relationships. In **horizontal analysis** percentage changes in financial statement items from one period to the next are calculated. In **vertical analysis** percentage relationships among the various items on the financial statements of one period are calculated.

ILLUSTRATION

Horizontal analysis:

Income Statement:

	19x2	19x1	Change from 19x1 to 19x2	
			Amount	Percent
Sales	$113,220	$102,000	$11,220	11
Sales returns	1,802	1,700	102	6

(Calculations for remaining income statement line items would be made in the same way. Calculations for the balance sheet items could also be made.)

The results of horizontal analysis can be used to identify areas in which unusual change has occurred. The amount of such changes and the related percentage of change provide an indication of the significance of the change.

ILLUSTRATION

Vertical analysis:

Balance sheet:

	19x2		19x1	
	Amount	Percent	Amount	Percent
Current assets:				
Cash	$ 38,600	12.9	$ 30,000	11.5
Short-term investments	3,000	1.0	1,000	0.4
Accounts receivable				
(net)	48,120	16.0	39,000	15.0
Total assets	$300,000	100.0	$260,000	100.0

(All balance sheet items would be stated as a percentage of total assets or total liabilities and equity. Income statement items would be stated as a percentage of net sales or total revenue.)

RATIO ANALYSIS

Numerous ratios can be calculated expressing relationships between two amounts. Such ratios provide information about liquidity or solvency, profitability, operating activity, and financial structure. The more common ratios used in financial statement analysis are listed below.

Ratios relating to liquidity or solvency:

Current ratio:

Current assets ÷ current liabilities

Quick (or acid-test) ratio:

Quick assets (cash, temporary investments, and accounts receivable) ÷ current liabilities

Ratios relating to profitability:

Earnings per share (calculated as required by **APB Opinion 15**)

Rate of return on assets:

Income before extraordinary items ÷ average total assets

Alternatively:

[Income before extraordinary items + interest expense (net of tax)] ÷ average total assets

Rate of return on stockholders' equity:

Income before extraordinary items ÷ average stockholders' equity

Price/earnings ratio:

Market price per share of common stock ÷ earnings per share

Profit margin (return on revenue):

Income before extraordinary items ÷ net sales (or total revenue)

Dividend payout ratio:

Cash dividends per share ÷ earnings per share

Alternatively:

Dividends declared ÷ number of shares of stock outstanding

Ratios relating to operating activity:

Receivables turnover:

Net credit sales ÷ average trade receivables (net)

Days sales in accounts receivable (age of accounts receivable):

Accounts receivable ÷ (sales ÷ 365 days)

Alternatively:

365 days ÷ receivables turnover

Inventory turnover:

Cost of goods sold ÷ average inventory

Days sales in inventory:

Inventory ÷ (cost of goods sold ÷ 365 days)

Turnover of assets:

Total revenue ÷ average total assets

Ratios relating to financial structure:

Debt to equity ratio:

Total debt ÷ total stockholders' equity

Debt to total assets ratio:

Total debt ÷ total assets

Times interest earned:

Income before interest expense, taxes, and extraordinary items ÷ interest expense